CONFRONTING THE CORRUPT

Dear Chris,

Paul Hoffman

CONFRONTING
THE CORRUPT

Accountability is the name of the game!

Best

Tafelberg

Tafelberg, an imprint of NB Publishers,
a division of Media24 Boeke Pty (Ltd),
40 Heerengracht, Cape Town, South Africa
www.tafelberg.com

Set in 10 on 15 pt Berkely
Cover by Nic Jooste
Book design by Nazli Jacobs
Edited by Riaan de Villiers
Proofread by Louise Brand
Commissioning editor: Gill Moodie

Printed and bound by Creda Communications,
Epping II, South Africa

First edition, first impression 2016

ISBN: 978-0-624-07768-8
Epub: 978-0-624-07769-5
Mobi: 978-0-624-07770-1

Dedication

FOR MY beautiful first-born daughter, Kate, who died too soon to see this book in print, but lived through most of the adventures it describes.

And for all the people of South Africa, poor, rich, and in-between, who sense in their hearts that a better life for all is best (and most sustainably) achieved by respecting the rule of law, promoting the rights in the Bill of Rights, and upholding the Constitution.

Let eternal vigilance be your watchwords for open, accountable, and responsive governance in our beloved country. Those who crafted our post-liberation order have identified these three values as foundational to our supreme law. Striving for their implementation is worth the effort.

Contents

Prologue

WHEN THE idea of creating an Institute for Accountability first hatched back in 2007, Jacob Zuma was a private citizen, the putsch of Polokwane had not yet happened, the arms deal was safely hidden under the well-worn carpet in Luthuli House. President Kgalema Motlanthe was yet to steer South Africa towards the 2009 general election after the resignation of President Thabo Mbeki in September 2008.

Much muddy water has flowed under the bridge since then. Some of the projects of the team at Accountability Now (the institute's new and more user-friendly name) have been completed, some are ongoing, and some will never end.

These disparate outcomes make it difficult to write a coherent account of the various ways in which corruption has been confronted. But there has to be a cut-off point, and ours arrived finally in July 2016. For more recent news, readers are encouraged to visit our website at www.accountabilitynow.org.za.

Acknowledgements

I WISH to thank the team at Accountability Now, especially our patron, 'The Arch', or Archbishop Emeritus Desmond Tutu, whose inspired efforts have played a vital role in turning the stories in this book into reality.

Next, this volume could not have taken shape without the dedicated effort of the Tafelberg team, who embraced the project and brought great skill to bear on the many tricky stages of the publishing process. It is invidious to single out individuals, and – given the controversial content of the book – this could harm their careers. You know who you are: a big thank you to one and all.

Despite his busy post-retirement schedule, the late Tim Dunne, a former chair of trustees at Accountability Now, read an early draft of the manuscript, and made valuable suggestions for improving it. His antipathy to the loose use of the words 'this' and 'these' and his suggestions for making the text more accessible to lay readers played a major role in shaping the eventual product.

Finally, and most importantly, I wish to thank my long-suffering wife, Elise, for putting up with me during the writing process. A distracted husband who rises at ludicrous hours to tap on his laptop, who lies in bed listening to ideas buzzing around in his head, and remains preoccupied for long periods with the many large and small challenges surrounding a project of this nature is not the type of husband contemplated by the 'for better' part of the matrimonial vows. With more books forming in my head, the worst may be yet to come . . . Without the love, understanding and support of family, writing a book is infinitely harder. I have enjoyed all three in bounteous measure throughout the process of writing this one.

'Power tends to corrupt, and absolute power corrupts absolutely.'

– Lord Acton, 5 April 1887

'There can be no gainsaying that corruption threatens to fell at the knees virtually everything we hold dear and precious in our hard-won constitutional order. It blatantly undermines the democratic ethos, the institutions of democracy, the rule of law, and the foundational values of our nascent constitutional project. It fuels maladministration and public fraudulence, and imperils the capacity of the state to fulfil its obligations to respect, protect, promote and fulfil all the rights enshrined in the Bill of Rights. When corruption and organised crime flourish, sustainable development and economic growth are stunted. And in turn, the stability and security of society is put at risk.'

– Deputy Chief Justice Dikgang Moseneke and
Justice Edwin Cameron, 17 March 2011

Preface

—·—

'Intelligent disobedience is about finding the healthy balance for living in a system with rules and authorities while maintaining our own responsibility for the actions we take. Doing right when what you are told to do, is wrong.'

– Ira Chaleff

THIS BOOK needs an explanatory preface more than most. I need to introduce readers to the anti-corruption work of the Institute for Accountability in Southern Africa (which campaigns as Accountability Now), explain why the institute exists, and why its personnel do what they do under its auspices.

It is certainly curious that an institute of this nature should have been established in 2009, a mere 15 years after South Africa was lauded internationally for its 'miraculous' transition to democracy, thereby inaugurating the shining hope of Archbishop Desmond Tutu's 'Rainbow Nation of God'. It is even stranger that seven stalwarts (three of whom are lawyers) have seen the need to serve as directors, and even more good folk have agreed, from time to time, to act as trustees of the institute, all without remuneration. Significantly, our patron is none other than Archbishop Emeritus Desmond Tutu. He has been a source of inspiration, a counsellor, and our moral guide.

It is also perplexing that the directors of Accountability Now are unpaid volunteers. With some noteworthy exceptions, whose moving spirits prefer to remain anonymous, there is little local appetite for funding so controversial a body. South Africa has also slipped off the radar screen of many international donor agencies, which no longer seem to regard it and its well-being as key to the future of sub-Saharan Africa. They are wrong. If the most advanced and sophisticated country in the sub-region degenerates into a kleptocracy, a kakistocracy or even – heaven forbid – a failed state, there is little hope for the rest of the continent. If, on the other hand, constitutionalism and the rule of law hold sway in South Africa, its democratic teething troubles are resolved, and the 'better life' for all promised by the post-apartheid order become a lived reality, sustainable development stands a better chance of becoming the lived reality of people elsewhere in the region. The presence of one Jacob Zuma in our national life looms large in this equation.

As an anonymous contributor to *The Economist* wrote in December 2015: 'The challenge for democrats will be to protect the independence of the courts, and what remains of other institutions. Mr Zuma has shown an inclination to wreck them. Unless checked, the danger is that when he goes, he will leave only the husk of democracy behind.'

Accountability Now exists to exact accountability from all those in positions of power or authority, not only in government. It also promotes responsiveness to the needs of ordinary people. These objectives are drawn from the foundational values set out in the South African Constitution of 1996. Accountability is central to the rule of law. Without effective checks on the exercise of power, an independent and unbiased judiciary, free media, an independent and vigorous civil society, and faith-based organisations that are prepared to 'hold feet to the fire', the rule of law will not thrive.

The most significant words in the 1955 Freedom Charter (the inspiration for much of the new constitutional order) are: 'The People Shall Govern'. There ought to be no confusion between ruling and governing. All too often, there is. The constitution is supreme, and everyone, including politicians and public servants, is ruled by its tenets and principles. It obliges the state to respect and protect human rights. Government by the people, through their elected representatives and civil servants, is also constrained by this simple yet effective arrangement. All government conduct and all laws made have to be consistent with the constitution. If they deviate from the constitutional standard, the courts will, upon complaint, strike down any and all of those inconsistencies as invalid. To the chagrin of those in government, this happens all too often.

Opposition political parties, 'Chapter Nine' institutions (institutions established under Chapter 9 of the constitution, including the Public Protector and Auditor General), faith-based organisations, business and industry, and all those who value their freedom have to be eternally vigilant about guarding the constitution, because it is our guarantor of freedom.

This book is the story of the modest contribution that Accountability Now has made to the constitutional project in South Africa by taking up the cudgels against corruption. It tells of the cases and causes the people of the institute have taken up, giving freely of their time and talents, to combat corruption and collusive dealings. In the oft-quoted words of the Constitutional Court:

'There can be no gainsaying that corruption threatens to fell at the knees virtually everything we hold dear and precious in our hard-won constitutional order. It blatantly undermines the democratic ethos, the institutions of democracy, the rule of law, and the foundational values of our nascent constitutional project. It fuels maladministration and public fraudulence, and imperils the capacity of the state to fulfil its obligations to respect, protect, promote and fulfil all the rights enshrined in the Bill of Rights. When corruption and organised crime flourish, sustainable development and economic growth are stunted. And in turn, the stability and security of society is put at risk.'

This passage, written in 2011 by then Deputy Chief Justice Dikgang Moseneke and Justice Edwin Cameron, would not have been written at all if Accountability Now had not assisted the Johannesburg businessman Bob Glenister in his campaign to save the Scorpions, the independent anti-corruption unit set up in 1999, and persuaded the Helen Suzman Foundation (HSF) to intervene as a friend of the court in the litigation that eventually led to the judgment in question. The 'conventionally wise' did not think the case could be won and, with the single exception of the HSF, declined to become involved. They were nearly right. The bench divided five to four – the narrowest possible margin of victory for Glenister, as the court from which the matter had emanated on appeal held the same opinion as the minority in the Constitutional Court.

Fighting corruption is not for sissies. It is risky, difficult, demanding, uncomfortable, and often unpopular (especially with the corrupt). Then why do it? This question is often asked, and admits no easy answer. Speaking truth to power, and using the machinery available to do so effectively, is lonely work. But it has to be done. A sense of social justice; concern about the trajectory of our beloved homeland, region and continent; an idealistic desire to make a difference, or to 'do one thing' to make the world a better place may go part of the way towards explaining the activities of Accountability Now. Its trustees, directors and staff are all acutely aware of the words of the anthropologist Margaret Mead, who famously said:

'Never doubt that a small group of thoughtful committed citizens can change the world; indeed, it's the only thing that ever has. Always remember that you are absolutely unique. Just like everyone else. Never believe that a few caring people can't change the world. For, indeed, that's all who ever have.'

Perhaps the hardest 'why' is this one: 'Why forsake your comfort zone to take up so thankless and difficult a task as combating corruption at this time and in this place?' Glib responses include:

'Because corruption is everywhere, and threatens all of us.'

'Because if we don't, who will?'

'Because we can.'

'Because it's the right thing to do.'

There are more subtle and more profound 'right/wrong' or 'good/evil' responses too: difficult to put in words, easier for some to intuit emotionally, yet always of a universally salutary nature. These are the replies that are felt in the heart, not spoken, put down on paper, or heard in one's mind. If they are not apparent yet, then read this book. It sets out to foster a better understanding of all the 'why' questions posed in this preface and their possible answers.

Glossary of acronyms and abbreviations

ANC: African National Congress political party

APC: Arms Procurement Commission, official name of the Seriti Commission

Armscor: Armaments Corporation of South Africa parastatal

BAe: British Aerospace, now known as BAe Systems

BRICS: Brazil, Russia, India, China, South Africa group

CRC: Children's Resource Centre

CFCR: Centre for Constitutional Rights

Cosatu: Congress of South African Trade Unions

COPE: Congress of the People political party

DA: Democratic Alliance political party

DIP: Defence Industrial Participation, part of the Department of Defence's policy framework for retention and development of the South African defence industry

DPCI: Directorate of Priority Crime Investigations, better known as 'the Hawks'

DPW: Department of Public Works

DSO: Directorate of Special Operations, better known as 'the Scorpions' and which was disbanded in 2009

ECAAR-SA: Economist Allied for Arms Reduction-South Africa

EFF: Economic Freedom Fighters political party

FF+: Freedom Front Plus political party

GCB: General Council of the Bar of South Africa, the professional body of advocates

HSF: Helen Suzman Foundation

IDASA: Institute for Democracy in South Africa

LIFT: Lead-in Fighter Training (that uses advanced jet trainer aircraft which emulate operational fighter planes)

LRC: Legal Resources Centre

LSSA: Law Society of South Africa, the professional body of attorneys

MP: Member of Parliament

NPA: National Prosecuting Authority

NIP: National Industrial Participation, Department of Trade and Industry's programme to grow and develop various economic sectors of South Africa

OECD: Organisation for Economic Co-operation and Development

OPP: Office of the Public Protector

PFMA: Public Finance Management Act

R2K: Right2Know campaign

RPF: Roux Property Fund

SAPS: South African Police Service

SAAF: South African Air Force

SAIRR: South African Institute of Race Relations

SANDF: South African National Defence Force

SCOPA: Standing Committee on Public Accounts (in South Africa's National Assembly)

SDPP: Strategic Defence Procurement Package, the official name of SA's arms deal

SFO: Serious Fraud Office (of the UK)

SIU: Special Investigating Unit

SJC: Social Justice Coalition of South Africa

SC: Senior Counsel or silk

STIRS: specialised, trained, independent, resourced and secure – criteria for effective corruption-busting initiatives as laid down by the Constitutional Court

TAC: Treatment Action Campaign

TRC: Truth and Reconciliation Commission

UDM: United Democratic Movement political party

Chapter 1
The early days

———•———

'The condition upon which God hath given liberty
to man is eternal vigilance.'
– John P Curran

LOOKING BACK at the watershed year of 2008 – when the idea of an Institute for Accountability in Southern Africa was first considered – is a bit like looking at a landscape through a telescope held the wrong way round. It's too close to the present to be history, and too distant to be the source of current news.

That was the year in which the palace revolution in the ranks of the African National Congress (ANC) made itself felt in South African politics. Much to their surprise and chagrin, Thabo Mbeki and his team were swept out of party-political office at the infamous ANC national conference held in Polokwane, Limpopo, in December 2007, with Mbeki losing the ANC presidency to Jacob Zuma.

The phrase 'Zuma tsunami', coined by Zwelenzima Vavi, then general secretary of the Council of South African Trade Unions (Cosatu), was on everyone's lips. With the help of the South African Communist Party, Cosatu, and the ANC Youth League, led by Julius Malema who, at that time, declared himself willing to 'kill for Zuma', there was indeed a tsunami within the Tripartite Alliance, and Zuma rose to power by a comfortable margin of 2 329 votes to 1 505, playing the role of innocent victim of a manipulative predecessor.

Nine months later, on 21 September 2008, Mbeki announced his resignation as South African president after being recalled by the national executive committee of the ANC, vacating the office he had inherited from the fabled Nelson Mandela a rattled man.

But tsunamis have their destructive side too. By 2015 the roles of the three men had morphed markedly: Zuma, now in his second term as national president, was 'Number One', and a 'Big Man' in BRICS, the loose alliance of Brazil, Russia, India and China to which South Africa has been added. Zuma was apparently close to the Russian president, Vladimir Putin, visited him frequently, and indications were that he would try to steer massive nuclear power procurements Russia's way. When Zuma fell ill, he travelled to Russia for medical treatment.

Malema, eventually expelled from the ANC for his fractiousness, was leading a two-year-old political party called the Economic Freedom Fighters (EFF), best known for its red-overalled members of parliament chanting 'Pay back the money!' in the National Assembly. This war-cry emanated from their demand that Zuma pay back undue personal benefits from state-sponsored upgrades to his country home at Nkandla in rural KwaZulu-Natal. The EFF commanded only 6 per cent of the popular vote, but had shaken up opposition politics. Vavi, caught in a honey trap and accused of corruption, had been deposed from any role in Cosatu, and ruefully admitted that he had erred in supporting Zuma.

The wry slogan 'No One is Above The Law' appeared on walls in urban landscape, saying at once that, in his efforts to avoid paying back the money, Zuma (aided and abetted by the ANC) was seeking to elevate himself above the law, and that, in a constitutional democracy, this was not supposed to happen. It was evident that the need to exact accountability and to promote responsiveness to the needs of ordinary people was as urgent in 2016 as it was back in 2008, even viewed through a telescope held the wrong way round.

In the spring of 2008, the Social Justice Coalition of South Africa (SJC), an organisation which grew out of the sterling efforts of Zachie Achmat's Treatment Action Campaign (TAC) for the state-sponsored treatment of HIV/AIDS, held a series of public meetings focusing on shortcomings in service delivery and other social justice issues relevant to the poor. Most meetings were held in Community House in Salt River, Cape Town, where experts, activists, and ordinary folk discussed mounting problems in areas ranging from education to health care and public transport.

The SJC invited a variety of speakers to inform the public in general and SJC members in particular about the current state of the nation, including deteriorating standards of governance, and the rapid and increasingly worrying spread of corruption. Given the success of the TAC in slaying the AIDS denialism dragon that had stalked the halls of government during the Mbeki presidency, expectations of the SJC spring campaign were high.

The final and biggest SJC meeting was held in St George's Cathedral in central Cape Town, a few metres from parliament, in November 2008. The cathedral is big enough to cope with the large crowd that the most popular topic in the series – the notorious Strategic Defence Procurement Package, or 'arms deal' – was bound to attract. The cathedral, widely known as 'the People's Cathedral', or just 'St Georges', has a long and proud history as a site of political and social engagement, and was therefore an appropriate venue for launching a campaign that culminated in a march on parliament in February 2009. The marchers were addressed from the back of an open truck by Max Price, Vice Chancellor of the University of Cape Town. They demanded the appointment of a commission of inquiry into the deals concluded by South Africa in 1999 with four European arms suppliers in circumstances that reeked of mal-feasance and misfeasance.

By then, Paul Holden, a young historian, had written an exposé called *The Arms Deal in Your Pocket* (Jonathan Ball, 2008), chronicling the perfidious behaviour that had sur-rounded the procurement process. The book exposed the of-fering of essentially bogus 'offset deals' as a sweetener for the massive sums of money spent on warplanes, submarines, frig-ates and helicopters for the perceived needs of a country with no military enemies, and no aggressive intentions.

Holden was the main speaker at the SJC meeting in the cathedral, and did not disappoint. Speaking with controlled pas-sion, he told the audience filling the pews and standing in the aisles what the money the government had borrowed for the arms deal would have achieved if it had been spent for socio-economic rather than defence purposes. It could have funded mass housing, public facilities such as schools and hospitals, and infrastructure such as roads, dams, and power supplies, creating thousands of jobs, and enabling further economic growth.

Instead, the government had entered into questionable loans it could ill afford to buy arms it did not need, to defend the country against enemies it did not have. Holden outlined irregularities in the financing and tender processes, pointed to evidence of bribery, and encouraged everyone present to sign the SJC petition addressed to then president Kgalema Motlanthe to use his powers under the constitution to appoint a commission of inquiry.

I was at the meeting in the cathedral, and at some of the earlier meetings too. At that time, I was the founding director of the Centre for Constitutional Rights (CFCR), a body formed to uphold the National Peace Accord that had informed the new constitutional dispensation which came into being in 1994. Unlike most others who attended the meetings, I had the privilege of being paid to attend them, in order to monitor the bedding down of constitutional democracy in Cape Town, including the roles played in protecting it by civil society. The CFCR prefers a non-confrontational and co-operative approach to discharging its mandate to uphold the constitution.

So I attended the basic education meeting at Community House with great interest. The keynote speaker, Dr Mampela Ramphele, then a World Bank director (this was before her belly-flop into party politics), caustically told the audience that the 'Bantu education' of her youth was better than the fare being dished up in the new South Africa.

It was also good to attend the public transport meeting at which my old client Les van Minnen spoke movingly. In June

2001, his son Jean was murdered on a train at Wynberg station in suburban Cape Town, giving rise to litigation by the Rail Commuters Action Group. The case led to a wise judgment by the Constitutional Court, delivered on 26 November 2004, that it is the duty of the rail authorities to take reasonable and accountable steps to secure the safety and security of passengers on their trains. The Rail Commuters case opened my eyes to the power of public interest litigation to improve the lives of ordinary people. It started with a phone call from an old school friend and tennis partner, Joe Frylinck:

'What will they do to me if I torch a couple of rail carriages at Fish Hoek station?' he asked with menace in his voice; a tone that showed that he was not joking.

'Joe, you will go to jail for arson; and I will come to Pollsmoor Prison to pass you peanuts through the bars,' I replied.

'Well', he retorted, 'we are fed up down here in Fish Hoek, and we expect accountability from Metrorail.'

When the Rail Commuters brief landed on my desk a few days later, I was a fairly jaded and cynical silk at the Cape Bar. My practice involved managing conflicts among the greedy, the angry and the stupid, provided they could afford my fees. The Rail Commuters Action Group could not afford senior counsel, but I decided to work for them on a contingency basis purely because of the justness of their cause. The case inspired me, and changed my life to such an extent that I left the Bar in May 2006 after 26 years (give or take a few stints as acting judge) to form the CFCR and start a new career in the non-profit sector, dedicated to promoting constitutionalism.

This change occurred after a long struggle on behalf of the

Rail Commuters Action Group that went through three courts, and consumed eight court days of argument. First, there were five days in the High Court (where they won handsomely), then one in the Supreme Court of Appeal (where they lost horribly), and, finally, two days in the Constitutional Court, where the accountability Joe had mentioned in our first conversation was eventually exacted.

By the spring of 2008, it was clear that I was not suited to the co-operative and non-confrontational style of the CFCR. Perhaps I had spent too many years litigating for a living to be completely weaned off the cut and thrust of court work, and to undertake mere 'friend of the court' interventions of the type the CFCR was then prepared to venture. Whatever the underlying reasons, I was working out an amicably agreed notice period in November 2008 when I heard Paul Holden speak in the cathedral.

Quite by chance, I found myself sitting next to Susannah Cowen, a feisty young junior at the Cape Bar with a penchant for public interest work. I had been her duly assigned mentor in my final years at the Bar, but her burgeoning practice and numerous junior briefs made my mentorship just about superfluous. Indeed, her meteoric rise made my slow and steady start at the Bar appear pedestrian by comparison.

Halfway through Holden's address, I turned to her to ask: 'If the president refuses to appoint the commission the SJC is asking for, surely that will be a reviewable decision?'

Susannah replied immediately: 'They would have to prove irrationality.'

To which I replied: 'Well, listen to what Holden is saying;

there is a lot in it that points to irrationality if no commission of inquiry is appointed.'

Susannah was not persuaded, but I was struck by the idea of litigating for the appointment of a commission of inquiry if the petition fell on deaf ears. Perhaps the light shining through the stained glass windows of the cathedral affected me in some way.

The cathedral was packed. However, in the front pew on the other side of the aisle, I saw a person I took from media photographs to be the peace activist Terry Crawford-Browne. He was a staunch member of the Anglican Church, which had given him the task of monitoring the Defence Review conducted by the South African government to establish its defence and armaments needs prior to the arms deals, and ought to have informed those deals, but sadly did not. Disturbed by what he had found, Terry had unsuccessfully litigated in the public interest over the validity of the loans that underpinned the arms deals, and had lost his entire retired banker's fortune in the process. An attempt to sequestrate his estate was thwarted when it came to light that, except for an ancient and rusty Fiat Uno, he had no assets that could be attached. Fortunately, his father-in-law had had the foresight to insist on an antenuptial contract that put the Crawford-Brownes' home in his wife's name.

After Paul Holden's speech, while the audience was filing out of the cathedral, I approached him with a question: 'What will you do if the president does not respond positively to your request for a commission of inquiry?'

Terry was within earshot, and came closer to hear the answer. Paul did not have one, and had obviously not yet thought about this. When I suggested that litigation to compel the appointment of a commission of inquiry might be an option, he baulked, pointed out how expensive that would be, looking sympathetically in Terry's direction. When I pointed out that contingency fee litigation does not have to be expensive, and that there may be lawyers who would be prepared to act on a 'no-win, no-pay' basis, Paul suggested that I meet Zachie Achmat.

Terry liked the idea of compelling a commission of inquiry, and immediately collaborated with me to consider what we could do to get the president to agree to a commission on the basis of the weight of support for the SJC petition.

Terry is close to Archbishop Desmond Tutu. His wife, Lavinia, served as the latter's secretary for many years, spanning his time as Archbishop of the Anglican Church in Southern Africa, and head of the Truth and Reconciliation Commission (TRC). The Arch and Terry worked on helping to bring down apartheid through the imposition of banking sanctions against the regime. It never came to that. Instead, on 2 February 1990, then president F W de Klerk announced sweeping reforms and the unbanning of the liberation movements, coupled with the release of political prisoners.

It seemed to us that getting F W de Klerk and the Arch to sign a letter supporting the appointment of a commission of inquiry would carry some weight in the Presidency.

So Terry and I sat down to draft a letter, asking for the appointment of a commission of inquiry, which we hoped both men would sign. They both did so within a few days of Terry and I first meeting on that fateful evening in the cathedral. Then, to our surprise, Helen Suzman and Mamphela Ramphele came forward of their own volition to sign the letter as well, which was sent off to the Presidency by hand in December 2008. It is hard to imagine four more disparate South African patriots: FW, the last leader of the apartheid state; Tutu, the controversial cleric; Ramphele, the black consciousness leader; and Suzman, the lone liberal parliamentarian in the darkest days of apartheid.

The president, then the 'caretaker' Kgalema Motlanthe, replied promptly. He noted the authors' concerns, but believed that if they had any evidence of criminality in the conclusion of the arms deals, they should report the matter to the police so that the country's anti-corruption unit – then the Directorate of Special Operations (DSO), or Scorpions – could deal with the complaint in the context of a criminal investigation.

This was rather ironic, as the government had already started taking steps to close down the Scorpions – the only effective anti-corruption unit in South Africa's history – and replace it with a Directorate for Priority Crime Investigation (DPCI), or Hawks, a police unit without the Scorpions' teeth, independence or tenacity. This dissolution was prompted by an 'urgent' resolution at the ANC's Polokwane conference in December 2007 which had swept Zuma into power, to the mortification of Mbeki and his supporters. They thought Mbeki was well set for a third term as ANC president despite the term limit as national president that would see him out of the Union Buildings after the election due in 2009.

The ANC secretary-general, Gwede Mantashe, did not mince his words when he explained why the Scorpions would be dissolved. They were taking too much interest in highly placed

ANC politicians, he explained to a gobsmacked Helen Zille, leader of the official opposition, the Democratic Alliance (DA), when she visited him at Luthuli House in Johannesburg in April 2008 to seek an explanation for the baffling decision to close down the highly functional Scorpions, located in the National Prosecuting Authority (NPA) instead of the South African Police Service (SAPS).

So, with the Scorpions on their way out and the Hawks not yet in place, it was not clear just how serious Motlanthe was when he invited us to report the malfeasance in the arms deals to the police. However, he had taken a clear decision not to appoint a commission of inquiry, and the rationality of that decision was open to attack under the doctrine of legality that underpins the rule of law.

None of the signatories to the letter, which effectively supported the SJC's petition, were in a position to supply relevant evidence, nor could they reasonably be expected to embark on intricate and controversial litigation against the president and the South African government. Who, then, would take up the cudgels?

Terry arranged a meeting with Zachie Achmat and his inner circle, which was held in the Long Street Café in Cape Town in December 2008. In order to create a positive atmosphere at the meeting, Terry indicated in advance that he would volunteer to be one of the claimants in the litigation necessary to reverse the president's decision.

Unfortunately, once Achmat was aware that Terry was gungho to sue, he lost interest in taking the litigation route, and invited Terry to press on alone. This reticence is quite understandable. As an indigent litigant, Terry did not need to fear an adverse costs award. This could not be said of the SJC or any of its individual representatives sitting at the table in the Long Street Café. There is a certain freedom in having no attachable assets, and Terry was prepared to exercise that freedom in further pursuing those suspected of skulduggery in the course of the arms deals. By then, Terry had also engaged his attorney of long standing, Charles Abrahams, to prepare the matter for court and to brief counsel to argue it.

We parted with the SJC on good terms, and in the knowledge that had their spring campaign not been organised, Terry and I would probably not have met at all, and the adventure upon which we were about to embark would not even have started.

So, from a chance meeting at a protest gathering in a famous cathedral grew the case of Terry Crawford-Browne versus the President of the Republic of South Africa and the Government of the Republic of South Africa, aimed at compelling the appointment of a commission of inquiry into malfeasance and misfeasance in the arms deals of 1999. Embarking on this course of action was a milestone, but planning the litigation was no easy task.

Chapter 2

To commission a commission

———•———

'Our Constitution is not merely a formal document regulating public power. It also embodies, like the German Constitution, an objective normative value system . . . it is within this matrix that the common law must be developed.'

– Justices Laurie Ackermann and Richard Goldstone

MY TIME at the CFCR ended at the end of 2008. My work there had always been part-time, initially for two and a half days a week, and later for three days a week. I was able to pursue other interests in my own time, and did so. During and after December 2008 my major preoccupation was to plan the case aimed at compelling the national president to appoint a commission of inquiry into the arms deals.

At this point, I think it will be helpful to describe the purpose of commissions of inquiry, and the processes involved in their appointment in terms of South African law. According to the editors of *LAWSA*, the encyclopaedic authority on South African law, the word 'commission' has two distinct meanings in the context of an inquiry. First, it refers to 'an authoritative charge or direction to act in a prescribed manner'. Second, it also refers to the body that carries out the charge or direction. In modern South African law, there are four kinds of commissions, namely executive, constitutional, statutory, and common law commissions. Terry Crawford-Browne and the SJC would try to compel the president, who has the power to do so in terms of the constitution, to appoint an executive commission of inquiry into the arms deals. This constitutional power is derived from the perogative of the sovereign in the pre-constitutional political order.

An executive commission is an instrument of policy-making for the benefit of the national executive: it is required to determine facts, and to make recommendations to the president as head of the executive. Neither the president, nor anyone else, is bound by the findings of fact or the recommendations of any commission. Although commissions are often presided over by judges, they are administrative in nature. The underlying idea is that a person as busy as the president, who is both the head of state and also head of the national executive, does not have the time to delve into a complex factual matrix in order to determine the truth, and make recommendations or even policy based upon the facts so determined.

A good example is the Marikana Commission of Inquiry, presided over by the retired appeal court judge Ian Farlam, which was tasked with investigating events at the Lonmin Platinum Mine at Marikana in North West in August 2012 which had resulted in the deaths of 44 people. This inquiry involved reams of evidence, the cross-examination of witnesses, and consideration of a great deal of expert opinion on the events that had unfolded during an unprotected strike by rock-drillers in search of better wages and living conditions. Clearly, no president could sit through the hearing of evidence and then sift through the material placed before the Farlam Commission, as the inquiry became known.

The process for appointing commissions is regulated in part by the Commissions Act of 1947. Procedures adopted by a commission must also comply with the provisions of the Promotion of Administrative Justice Act of 2000.

The first question that had to be considered in preparing the case that Terry was prepared to launch was the nature of the relief to be claimed in the matter. While many lawyers would have plumped for a review of the presidential decision to refuse the request by the SJC and the four prominent citizens, we decided that an order compelling the president to appoint a commission, or an order directing him to reconsider the refusal of the request, would be a more streamlined approach. We bore in mind that Motlanthe was a 'bench-warmer' or temporary president who would be replaced by the president of the ANC in the likely event of the ANC winning the general elections to be held in May 2009. This would mean that by the time the matter came to court, a different president – probably Zuma – would be in office.

This created all sorts of complications for the intended litigation, notably that Zuma's former financial adviser, one Schabir Shaik, had been convicted in 2005 of corrupting Zuma, inter alia in relation to the arms deals. In the course of that case, it was proven beyond reasonable doubt that a South African subsidiary of the French arms and electronics manufacturer Thomson, later known as Thint, which had provided the combat suites for the navy corvettes, had paid Zuma R500 000 a year. These payments were made to encourage Zuma to use his position as deputy president and leader of government business in parliament to protect Thomson against investigations of the arms deal bidding process, and helping it to secure further government contracts. While Shaik's conviction did not bind or directly affect Zuma, it would place him in a rather awkward position.

Then there was the question of which court to approach for the relief which we would decide to seek. One option was a direct approach to the Constitutional Court, the highest court in the land. At that time, the learning in law on the topic of direct approaches to this court, which has a distinct preference for sitting as a court of final appeal rather than a court of first instance, was complicated, opaque and contradictory.

We approached learned professors in this field for their advice. Both Pierre de Vos at the University of Cape Town and George Devenish at the University of KwaZulu-Natal advised us not to approach the Constitutional Court directly. That left Terry with a choice between the High Courts in Pretoria and Cape Town. The former is the administrative capital of the country, and the latter the legislative capital. This arrangement had begun with the Union of South Africa in 1910, and did not change with the advent of a constitutional democracy in 1994. As he lives in Cape Town, Terry was content to sue in the High Court there, simply as a matter of convenience and because the president had a suitable address for service, namely De Tuynhuys, his official Cape Town residence, which is situated in the Gardens right next to parliament.

Next, it was necessary to decide whether to proceed by way of action or application. An action is the better legal route in matters of this nature when it is apparent that disputes of fact may arise. An application is usually decided on the respondent's version of events, taken together with whatever is not disputed in the applicant's founding papers. Given that the arms deal cover-up was already a thriving cottage industry among organs of state and politicians, we expected some of Terry's factual allegations to be hotly disputed. This meant that we would need to proceed by way of an action, in which evidence could be led and tested under cross-examination.

There was another good reason to proceed by way of action. Publicly available information suggested strongly that at least some of the bribes paid by arms manufacturers in order to secure the contracts were used to pay for the ANC's 1999 election campaign, and strengthen its coffers in general. We thought this could be confirmed by serving the ANC treasurer-general with a subpoena ordering him to bring its financial records to court, so that its donors could be identified and compared with the individuals and organisations implicated in the skulduggery swirling around the arms deals. In this way, the malfeasance could be established via a paper trail rather than the arduous business of cross-examining witnesses in the course of a trial.

So the business of preparing particulars of claim for issue out of the Western Cape High Court began in earnest, once the advice of the professors and the tactical considerations had been carefully weighed. We decided on a bare bones-type of pleading so as to make it as difficult as possible for the president to deal with the meat of the case in the course of his written response. It is never good practice to plead evidence.

After much drafting and redrafting, in which my junior in this case, Peter Hazell SC, played an enthusiastic role, the core of the claim took the following form. I cite this at some length, as it provides a useful summary of the arms deal and the subsequent allegations of corruption.

On or about 3 December 1999, the South African government signed a set of contracts in terms of which it agreed to buy three submarines from the German Submarine Consortium; four frigates from the German Frigate Consortium; 30 utility helicopters from Agusta; 24 Hawk trainer aircraft from BAe; and 28 Saab Gripen JAS39 fighter aircraft from BAe/Saab.

One or more or all of these contracts were tainted by fraud, corruption or other irregularities which justified the cancellation of the contracts and the recovery of all amounts paid. This assessment was based on a range of facts and allegations which were already publicly known. These included:

- Information contained in three books about the arms deals, written by Terry Crawford-Browne, Andrew Feinstein and Paul Holden;
- The conviction of former ANC chief whip Tony Yengeni on charges of fraud, arising from the fact that he had bought a Mercedes-Benz sports utility vehicle at a discount arranged by one of the subcontractors to an arms dealer;
- The conviction in the Durban High Court of Schabir Shaik, former financial adviser to Jacob Zuma, and ten companies under his control on charges of fraud and corruption relating to payments made to Zuma in which arms deal interests were implicated;

- Charges then pending against Zuma relating to his acceptance of money from Thint, a company involved in one of the arms deals, allegedly in return for protecting it against investigation;
- Zuma's verbal threat, made in March 2008, that if he was convicted on those charges, he would expose others;
- Judge Chris Nicholson's recommendation that a commission of inquiry into the arms deal be appointed, made in the course of his judgment in the case between Zuma and the National Prosecuting Authority (NPA) in the Natal High Court on 12 September 2008;
- Criminal proceedings against and investigations of various individuals and companies in respect of alleged bribery and corruption related to the South African arms deals in foreign jurisdictions;
- The findings of a joint investigating team comprising the Public Protector, the Auditor General and the National Director of Public Prosecutions in a report dated 14 November 2001 that raised suspicions of misfeasance and malfeasance in respect of the arms deals;
- The results of an investigation into the arms deals conducted by the parliamentary Standing Committee on Public Accounts (SCOPA), which did likewise; and
- The dossier about the arms deals tabled in parliament by Patricia de Lille, MP, on 9 September 1999.

Second, we argued that the arms deals were economically and legally irrational. Initially, the government had stated it would spend R 30.3 billion in return for offset deals worth R104 billion, which would include creating 65 000 jobs. However, the costs of the arms deals had increased from R30.3 billion to more than R50 billion, despite the fact that in August 1999 an Affordability Team reporting to a Ministers' Committee on the Affordability of the Defence Strategic Armaments Packages had recommended that expenditure should not exceed R16.5 billion, and that the benefits related to the acquisitions were 'not nearly as certain as their costs'.

As anticipated by the Affordability Team, all or most of the offset deals, including the 65 000 jobs, had not materialised. As a result, we argued, the costs of the arms deals far outweighed current or any future benefits. There was no current or future threat to national security against which the purchased arms could possibly be used. Moreover, the arms bought were either useless or underutilised.

Third, we argued that the arms deals contravened the constitution in that the procurement process was not fair, equitable, transparent, competitive or cost-effective, and should therefore be set aside. Additional points made included:

The stated costs of R30.3 billion did not include the costs of loan finance; appropriate provision for currency exchange rate fluctuations; and appropriate provision for the effects of inflation.

In November 2008, some of the assets of Fana Hlongwane, an adviser to the then Minister of Defence, the late Joe Modise, were frozen by court order due to his involvement in corrupt dealings and illegal commissions.

In August 2008, the *Sunday Times* reported that former president Thabo Mbeki had received a bribe of R30 million, of which he had passed on R28 million to the ANC, and R2 million to

Zuma. Despite being quick to do so in other instances, neither Mbeki nor Zuma instituted defamation or any other proceedings in respect of these allegations.

In 2008, the ANC embarked on its own fact-gathering exercise about the arms deals, ostensibly to inform its post-Polokwane leadership. The findings of this exercise were never made public.

In a report released in January 2009, the Independent Panel Assessment of Parliament stated that parliament should continue to exercise oversight over the arms deals, and take whatever steps it deemed necessary to pursue this matter, including debating a resolution calling for the appointment of a judicial commission of inquiry.

On 16 January 2009, the SCOPA chairman, Themba Godi, complained publicly that the attempts of his committee to obtain information about the arms deals from government departments, Armscor, and the NPA had been rebuffed. Godi threatened to summons the NPA, Armscor, and the Department of Trade and Industry to appear before his committee, declaring: 'If they can't write, perhaps they can talk'.

On 20 August 2008, the plaintiff (Terry Crawford-Browne) laid criminal complaints concerning perjury in the cover-up of impropriety in the arms deals. These claims related to statements made under oath by Trevor Manuel, Minister of Finance at the time of the arms deals, and Maria Ramos, then director general of the National Treasury, who later became Manuel's wife, in the earlier litigation aimed at cancelling the loans that underpinned the arms deals.

In a letter dated 28 March 2008, a businessman, Richard Young, asked the NPA to investigate corruption in respect of the arms deals. He claimed his company was a victim. Subsequent to his letter, the government paid Young's company, CCII, a settlement of R15 million.

In a letter dated 26 January 2007, Economists Allied for Arms Reduction-South Africa (ECAAR-SA), chaired by Terry Crawford-Browne, drew the attention of the Public Protector to alleged wrongdoing in the arms deals. Despite these requests and initiatives, no discernible progress had been made in investigating these issues.

In formulating our allegations, we tried to prevent legal point-taking as well as the taking of exceptions. The latter procedure allows defendants to object to documents submitted by claimants on the grounds that they are 'vague and embarrassing', in the quaint terminology of the Rules of Court, or do not disclose a 'cause of action'. Claimants either have to amend the documents in question, or face dismissal of their claims. As can be expected, the 'exception route' is often taken by litigants who are reluctant to deal with the merits of the claim. But our efforts to avoid this came to nought.

The president's legal team took exception after exception with a view to stringing out the case, in the apparent hope that Terry would either lose interest, or die before the case got to court. But Terry is made of sterner stuff than that, so we dealt with the technical point-taking as best we could, with a view to bringing the matter to a head sooner rather than later.

Eventually, after much paper skirmishing, the president's legal team, then led by Marumo Moerane SC, ran out of 'vague and embarrassing' points and filed a more substantive exception to the effect that the matter should be heard in the Constitutional

Court rather than the High Court. While this contradicted the advice we had received from the two learned professors, we took a tactical decision to concede the point and take Terry's complaint to the highest court, which the president seemed to prefer. Any other route would have involved lengthy technical wrangling, which is exactly what the president wanted, and Terry wanted to avoid.

The parties could not agree on who should bear the costs of the High Court action thus far. The matter was allocated to Acting Judge Nonkosi Saba, who had been elevated to this temporary position from the Magistrates' Court. She curtsied politely when the two teams met and greeted her before the hearing. It must have been the highlight of her acting stint, which did not lead to a permanent appointment. Acting Judge Saba would not have been exposed to so many grizzled advocates and so many constitutional issues in any hearing over which she had previously presided. The humour displayed by the Judge President of the Western Cape High Court, John Hlophe, in allocating this weighty matter to an acting judge with so little experience was not lost on the legal teams.

Terry's team argued that, given that this was a public interest matter that would not benefit him personally, it would be inappropriate for him to bear the costs of the aborted High Court action, which he could ill afford. The president's team argued, in turn, that the usual rule should apply and that Terry, having effectively abandoned his High Court action, should be made to pay its costs.

Since then, the Constitutional Court has clarified the law on this sticky issue. Following its landmark 2009 judgment in the

Biowatch case, litigants seeking to advance the public interest or to assert their rights under the Bill of Rights are not required to pay the defendants' costs if their case does not succeed – provided their claims are not found to be frivolous or vexatious.

Acting Judge Saba did not have the benefit of the Biowatch decision. She decided instead that the question of costs should stand over for determination after the matter had been heard in the Constitutional Court. This never happened; the president eventually abandoned his claim for costs against Terry in terms of a settlement agreement concluded between the attorneys representing both parties.

Chapter 3

The arms deal goes to Braamfontein

—————

'The servile will is the will that makes itself a slave to authority. It diminishes human nature.'
– Paul Ricoeur

PREPARING THE case for the Constitutional Court involved a complete tactical revision. Before dealing with this, it will be useful to recount what the court is meant to do, and how it goes about its business. The following summary is drawn largely from the court's own website.

The Constitutional Court deals exclusively with final appeals and constitutional matters – those cases that raise questions about the application or interpretation of the constitution. A case can reach it in one of four ways: as the result of an appeal against a judgment of the High Court or the Supreme Court of Appeal; by way of a direct application, asking it to sit as a court of first and last instance because of the urgency of the matter; when a lower court declares a piece of legislation invalid, which requires confirmation by the Constitutional Court; or when the president asks it to review a Bill. The court has the discretion to decide whether or not it will hear a matter, except when an Act has already been declared invalid, and the court is required to confirm the finding.

Typically, cases that reach the Constitutional Court start in the High Court, which has the power to grant various remedies and can declare legislation invalid. Any decision that invalidates provincial or parliamentary legislation or any conduct of the president must be confirmed by the Constitutional Court before it has any effect.

If the High Court rules against an application, the Constitutional Court may be approached on appeal. Applicants must show that the case concerns a constitutional matter. The Constitutional Court judges will decide if an important principle relating to the interpretation of the Constitution has been raised, and consider whether there is a reasonable prospect that the appeal may succeed.

If the court decides to grant leave to appeal, or wishes to hear argument about whether leave to appeal should be granted, the case is set down for a certain date so that argument from the parties can be heard. Each party submits written submissions before the date of argument so that the judges can familiarise themselves with the case and the position taken by each party. Sometimes, other interested parties may ask to be joined in proceedings, or be admitted as an *amicus curiae* (friend of the court). They too will make written submissions and sometimes give oral argument, if directed by the Chief Justice to do so.

As regards direct access, the constitution allows a person, 'when it is in the interests of justice and with leave of the Constitutional Court', to bring a matter directly to the Constitutional Court, or to appeal directly to the Constitutional Court from any other court. This is only allowed in exceptional circumstances.

Matters are heard by a quorum of at least eight judges. Usually, all eleven judges hear every case. The court does not hear evidence, or question witnesses. As it functions largely as a court of appeal, it considers the evidence heard in the original court that heard the matter. As a result, the court works largely with written arguments presented to it. The hearings are intended to address difficult issues raised by those arguments.

Once a case has been set down, the Chief Justice will ask a particular judge to prepare for it, and possibly write the judgment. Usually cases will be spread out, so that each judge writes a judgment from time to time. Once all parties have been heard, the judges meet to discuss the possible outcome of the case.

Writing a judgment is a long process. The assigned judge prepares a first draft, and circulates it. The judges then meet, and submit comments or changes. If a dissenting judgment has been written, the judges will begin to indicate which judgment they will follow, and why. Sometimes, lengthy discussions take place. Once consensus is reached, the judgments are thoroughly checked. The judgment is then handed down, or released, at a public sitting of the court.

Applications for direct access to the Constitutional Court take the form of a notice of motion, supported by an affidavit which sets out the facts which the applicant relies on for relief. The applications are lodged with the Registrar, and served on all parties with a direct or substantial interest in the relief claimed. The applications set out why the applicant believes granting the order to direct access is in the interests of justice; the nature of the relief sought, and the grounds upon which such relief is based; whether the matter can be dealt with by the court without hearing oral evidence; and if it can't, how such evidence should be adduced and conflicts of fact resolved.

Parties wishing to oppose the application are required to notify the applicant and the Registrar of their intention to do so. The Chief Justice may then call on the respondents to make written submissions to the court about whether or not direct access should be granted; or indicate that no written submissions or affidavits need be filed.

Given all this, Terry not only had to motivate why the court should grant his plea, but why it should consider the matter at all. Specifically, the particulars of claim had to be refashioned into an affidavit, submitted by Terry, asking the court to order the current president to appoint a commission of inquiry, or to reconsider the decision of his predecessor, Kgalema Motlanthe, not to do so, and explaining why he believed the court should hear the matter. It was October 2010, a long haul and many moons after the initial spark of inspiration in the 'People's Cathedral' almost two years earlier.

Terry's legal team decided that a lean and mean approach was still indicated. The particulars of claim were attached to the affidavit, together with a timeline of the activities around the arms deals drawn from Paul Holden's book *The Arms Deal in your Pocket*.

In the affidavit, Terry stated that the president had thwarted his attempt to litigate the matter in the High Court, but that he was prepared to return there if ordered to do so. Preparing the matter for trial to the point at which the plaintiff could issue a subpoena compelling the ANC to produce its financial records and the report on its internal inquiry into the arms deals was one of Terry's primary goals. This was the one thing the presidential legal team wanted to avoid above all else.

It may be that the president decided to avoid the High Court hearing in the hope that Terry could not afford a Constitutional Court hearing, and would be put off by the effort involved. In subsequent cases, the president adopted topsy-turvy stances in relation to jurisdiction. When Fred Daniel, who dreams of creating a trans-frontier national park near Badplaas in Mpumalanga, went directly to the Constitutional Court to ask for a commission of inquiry into corruption in that province, he was told to start in the High Court. When, in August 2012, the Marikana widows went to the High Court in an attempt to compel the president to release the Farlam Commission report he had received in March, the president argued that the High Court did not have jurisdiction. Such are the gyrations of political expediency.

In Terry's case, the notice of application and founding affidavit were duly filed in the Constitutional Court soon after the president had argued that the High Court did not have the power to entertain Terry's claims. Stripped of excess verbiage and procedural waffle, Terry's affidavit stated the following:

He had instituted the High Court action after the current president's predecessor had refused the request for the appointment of a commission of inquiry by Archbishop Emeritus Desmond Tutu and former president F W de Klerk. The pleadings in this action were not yet closed. The president had filed exceptions that required amendments to the original claim. Following these amendments, the president filed a further exception, arguing that the matter should be heard in the

Constitutional Court. Even if this was incorrect, Terry argued, the interests of justice would be served by gaining direct access to the Constitutional Court. Reasons included:

- Continued litigation about the exceptions would create long delays in getting to grips with the real issues. This would not serve the public interest, or the interests of justice.
- Adherence to the rule of law was a foundational value of South Africa's constitutional democracy, and required functionaries of state, including the president, to discharge their constitutional obligations and responsibilities in a fair and accountable manner.
- The factual matrix underpinning his case, as set out in the Amended Particulars of Claim, was replete with evidence and allegations that 'cried out for proper investigation', with a view to bringing anyone guilty of criminal activity to justice. Even if some or all of the allegations were ill-founded, the mere fact that they existed justified the appointment of a commission of inquiry.
- If any wrongdoing was uncovered, the relevant arms deals could be cancelled, and the South African government could claim damages in terms of escape clauses in the relevant contracts. In any case, under the common law, the government could withdraw from the deals in question, and claim restitution. This would save billions of rands in public funds which could be put to better use than buying unnecessary and unsuitable arms.

The scourge of corruption needed to be addressed if South Africa's constitutional democracy was to survive. The president, the government and the ANC had repeatedly declared that addressing corruption was one of the country's top priorities. In reality, public resources, time and energy had been 'massively squandered' on attempted cover-ups of the arms deal scandal.

'Unless and until a proper, independent and thorough investigation is undertaken,' Terry declared, 'the allegations of irregularities, fraud and corruption will remain unaddressed, to the detriment of the people of South Africa and those against whom the allegations are directed. The credibility of leading politicians and the viability of constitutional democracy and good governance are also threatened by the failure to appoint a commission of inquiry.'

He also noted the following:

On 4 October 2010, Colonel Johan du Plooy, the only member of the DPCI still working on the arms deals investigations, informed him that the head of DPCI, Major-General Anwa Dramat, had closed the police investigations into the BAe and German frigate consortium arms deals four days previously. This was a perplexing decision, as Saab had been charged in the Swedish courts with corruption arising out of its role in the BAe arms deal.

Until the demise of the Scorpions, the British Serious Fraud Office (SFO) and the South African NPA had collaborated closely with one another – to the point where, in November 2008, the Pretoria High Court granted an order allowing the Scorpions to search premises in Cape Town and Gauteng owned by or linked to Fana Hlongwane, former adviser to the late defence minister Joe Modise, and the Zimbabwean arms trader and businessman John Bredenkamp. This followed long-running SFO investigations into the BAe deal which had uncovered large payments to Hlongwane and Bredenkamp, while they were in a position to influence the award of the R21 billion contract.

On 7 September 2010, DPCI representatives told SCOPA that the Scorpions had handed over 460 boxes and 4.7 million computer pages of evidence against BAe. The seizure of documentation in November 2008 was public knowledge. This had preceded and motivated the joint appeal by Archbishop Tutu and former President De Klerk to the former president for a judicial commission of inquiry.

Documents in his (Terry's) possession included 166 pages of affidavits by Scorpion and SFO officials detailing how BAe had paid bribes totalling £115 million to secure its contracts, to whom the bribes were paid, and into which bank accounts. If necessary, these papers would be made available to the Constitutional Court.

On 8 February 2010, he had written to the president, urging him to deal with the irregularities in the arms deals or appoint a commission of inquiry. The president did not respond.

On 6 August 2010, he had written a detailed letter to SCOPA, asking it to request the president to appoint a judicial commission of inquiry into BAe's payment of bribes in order to secure its contracts with South Africa. Given the 'remedies in case of bribes' clause in the BAe contracts, the commission should consider whether Armscor and/or the government should cancel the contracts, and claim compensation.

He (Terry) had attended a SCOPA meeting on this issue on

7 September 2010. The 'disinterested and defensive' attitude of a majority of its members confirmed that there was no political will either in parliament or in the DPCI to investigate the arms deal. Indeed, SCOPA's attitude and the decision by the DPCI to close its investigations made a mockery of any stated intentions by those in power to address allegations of corruption.

'I have also brought this matter to the attention of the Public Protector,' Terry wrote, 'but have received no response. I therefore affirm that all other fora have been investigated and exhausted.'

Much water had flowed under the bridge since the arms deals were concluded. Many of the potential witnesses were no longer young or well. (Shabir Shaik, for example, was on medical parole due to a medical finding that he was terminally ill.) There was also much documentation, some of which was in jeopardy of being lost or destroyed, which any conscientious commission of inquiry would want to consider. It was therefore appropriate to afford the matter a degree of priority, in the public interest.

Dramat's decision to close the police investigations might lead to the precipitate and unfortunate destruction of documents in the possession of the police which were vital to getting to the truth of the allegations in the amended particulars of claim. Terry's Cape Town attorney had written to Dramat to request that all documentation in the possession of the police be preserved, pending the final determination of this matter. No response had been received.

Given the evidence as set out in detail in the amended particulars of claim, Terry wrote, it was 'illegal and irrational' for the president to have failed or refused to appoint a commission of inquiry, and asked the court to instruct the president to do so. He also asked the court to enable the hearing of evidence in Europe from relevant arms suppliers, politicians, and those involved in the investigations and prosecutions then in progress in Europe.

A breathless wait for directions from the court followed the filing of the application. We did not have to wait long. On 30 November 2010, the court ordered the president and government to file affidavits responding to the application for direct access by Tuesday 7 December 2010. Terry now had a toe-hold on being heard. The court had not rebuffed him without a hearing (as happens often, and happened to Fred Daniel later when he sought the same kind of relief as Terry).

In the event, the affidavits filed in response to the court's directions were disappointing. The president made no effort to deal with the substance of the application. Instead, as in the High Court, he presented a range of technical arguments, even going so far as to suggest that the High Court was the appropriate venue for the case. This was really rich, coming from the same legal team that had argued earlier that the High Court had no right or jurisdiction to hear the matter.

On 7 February 2011, the Constitutional Court set the matter down for hearing on 5 May 2011, and asked for written and oral arguments in response to the following questions:

- Under what circumstances is the Constitutional Court empowered to scrutinise the exercise by the president of his constitutional power to appoint a commission of inquiry?
- Does the constitution oblige the president to exercise this

power whenever there are indications of corruption, malfeasance, and misfeasance in relation to public procurement?

- If not, in what circumstances do indications of corruption, malfeasance and misfeasance oblige the president to appoint a commission of inquiry?
- More particularly, in the circumstances alleged by the applicant, and assuming that all his allegations are true, does it follow that the president is constitutionally obliged to exercise his power to appoint a commission of inquiry?
- If so, what steps should the court take to resolve disputes of fact? If not, is the court able to dispose of the application without resolving disputes of fact?

Peter Hazell and I thought long and hard about these questions. The success or failure of the case would depend on how we answered them. We eventually decided we should say that a president who irrationally refused to appoint a commission when asked on sound grounds to do so should be subjected to the scrutiny of the courts for conduct inconsistent with the constitution. This argument is based on the supremacy of the rule of law in the constitution, and the invalidity of conduct that infringes the doctrine of legality, which requires rationality in decision-making in that decisions taken should serve a legitimate purpose of government. Any refusal to appoint a commission of inquiry into an issue that cried out for investigation would, we thought, fit the criteria for being struck down as invalid by the courts.

This argument does not mean that any such situation would necessitate a commission. A complaint to the Public Protector, the Human Rights Commission, or even the police may suffice in a situation in which the facts are known or not concealed, and a clear-cut case can be made. If, however, as was apparent in respect of the arms deals, malfeasance and misfeasance are covered up, a commission is indicated. Whether or not a commission should be appointed would depend on the rationality of the refusal to appoint. We were back at the point Susannah Cowen had raised in St George's Cathedral after Paul Holden's address more than two years previously.

Lastly, we argued that it was not necessary to resolve disputes of fact; their existence was enough to justify the appointment of a commission of inquiry. Alternatively, they could be resolved by a commissioner, or referred back to the Western Cape High Court.

The president, not unexpectedly, had a very different take on the matter, which emerged from the rather sparse heads of argument filed on his behalf. In essence, they argued that the president was not obliged to appoint a commission of inquiry whenever there were indications of corruption, malfeasance and misfeasance in relation to public procurement, and could assign the task of dealing with such allegations to other state agencies, which he had done in respect of the arms deals. These measures could only be challenged if they were irrational or otherwise inconsistent with the constitution, which was not the case in this instance. This would still be the case even if the applicant could prove all his allegations. As a result, issues around resolving disputes of fact did not arise.

In our heads of argument, we dealt with the questions at far greater length. We submitted we had to show that the president's refusal to appoint a commission of inquiry was irrational, but could in fact do so. Grounds for stating this included the following:

No official investigation of the arms deal was currently in progress. In the light of the convictions of Yengeni and Shaik, the investigation of Zuma, and the criminal investigations in Europe of the same arms deals and dealers, it was clear that the rule of law would be negatively impacted if these allegations of corruption were true.

The DSO, or Scorpions, the last state institution to seriously investigate the arms deal, was disbanded in July 2009. The last person with the authority and personal independence to drive such an inquiry was the national director of public prosecutions, Vusi Pikoli, who was suspended in September 2007 and eventually dismissed without good reason. None of his successors had displayed his appetite to act without fear, favour or prejudice in investigating the arms deals.

The DSO's successor, the DPCI, had closed its files. Yet it was the only unit which could theoretically investigate criminality in respect of the arms deals. As the inquiry involved both criminal and civil law, an independent commission of inquiry was the only rational means of investigating both aspects.

The Public Protector had not responded to an approach by the applicant dated 30 August 2010. The Standing Committee on Public Accounts in Parliament had been thwarted by the DPCI decision to close its files, and by the general unwillingness of the national director of public prosecutions to investigate the matter. There had been no response to the applicant's letter to the chairman of SCOPA dated 6 August 2010. The fact that the post-Polokwane ANC leadership had held an internal inquiry into the arms deals but has not made the findings public was significant, in that a clean bill of health would surely have been publicised.

In these circumstances,' we wrote, 'the inference is inescapable that there is no political will accountably and openly to get to grips with the allegations of impropriety surrounding the arms deals. By compelling an inquiry, this court will immeasurably enhance the public confidence it already enjoys, and will bolster its legitimacy as the main bulwark against the abuse of power by serving the law and the constitution as a check on the incorrect and improper exercise of procedural executive power which is inherent in the refusals to appoint a commission of inquiry in circumstances which cry out for the appointment to be made.'

The circumstances sketched in the papers filed and referred to earlier created a factual matrix that made it patently irrational to fail or refuse to appoint a commission of inquiry. 'The failure of the criminal justice administration, the Office of the Public Protector, and SCOPA to get to grips with the serious allegations of corruption, malfeasance and misfeasance which were first aired in parliament as long ago as 9 September 1999 is reason enough to oblige a president acting in terms of the rule of law and the precepts of legality, rationality and fairness to appoint a commission of inquiry.'

Given the unusual (perhaps unique) circumstances of the case, an independent commission of inquiry was the only rational means of investigating the criminal as well as civil ramifications of the allegations of corruption, malfeasance and misfeasance in the course of the arms procurement process.

'It would be irrational and therefore unconstitutional for the president to persist in the failure and refusal to appoint a commission of inquiry in the face of the mountain of evidence contained in the founding papers filed by him, read with the three books, court records, judgments and records of investigation to which he refers as part of the allegations of fact.'

We argued that the questions surrounding possible factual disputes could not be addressed before it became clear whether the president would dispute any of the facts and allegations, which he had not yet done. Accordingly, we asked the court to order the president to file an affidavit responding to the substance of the applicant's claims.

We waited, hoping that the president (unlikely) or the court (perhaps) would respond to the informal invitation for the president to deal with the substance of Terry's affidavit. When there was no movement on the issue, we launched a formal application which the president opposed and the court did not deal with prior to the scheduled date for hearing of 5 May 2011. The table was accordingly decked for a battle royal.

In the run-up to the hearing, we received comfort and succour from a welcome ally. The South African Institute of Race Relations, whose then director, John Kane-Berman, had long advocated the appointment of a commission of inquiry into the arms deals, decided to intervene as an *amicus curiae*, or friend of the court. Prof Max du Plessis led the legal team assembled for the intervention, and my old Wits University classmate Anthea Jeffery, head of research at the SAIRR, submitted a supporting affidavit. Two sections of the heads of argument of the *amicus* are noteworthy; the first discussed the effects of corruption, and the second responded to the questions posed by the Chief Justice in his practice note.

On the threat of corruption to the constitutional order, the heads of argument stated that both the Constitutional Court and the Supreme Court of Appeal had emphasised that corruption threatened the rule of law, good governance, democracy, and fundamental rights. International conventions also recognised that that corruption undermined accountability, transparency, and governments' ability to provide basic services. South Africa's own legislation, in the form of the Prevention and Combating of Corrupt Activities Act, acknowledged that corruption undermined rights, the credibility of governments, democracy, morality, and the rule of law.

In the recent Glenister case, both the majority and the minority judgments of the Constitutional Court had identified corruption as a scourge which posed a grave danger to democracy, accountability, the rule of law, and guaranteed human rights.

Among other things, the court held that endemic corruption threatened the injunction that government must be accountable, responsive and open; that public administration must not only be held to account but must also be governed by high standards of ethics and efficiency, and must use public resources in an economic and effective way. As regards public finance, the constitution demanded budgetary and expenditure processes marked by openness, accountability and effective financial management. Similar requirements applied to public procurement, when organs of state contracted for goods and services.

In the Glenister case, the Constitutional Court had defini-
tively recognised the effects of corruption on the life of a nation,
its laws, and the rights of all its people; its ability to decimate
hard-earned freedoms; and its insidious nature, and held that
the state had the duty to root it out.

'The *amicus* submits that Glenister is an essential prism
through which to view the present matter ... the arms deal
and the corruption associated with it from the outset, (some
alleged, some already proven in court) has become a central and
debilitating feature of our political life. The public, the government, and those implicated by allegations of impropriety
deserve for the truth to be uncovered.'

The respondents' obligation to seek the truth about alleged
corrupt activities was ultimately sourced in the constitution,
and the state's constitutional duty to fight corruption. In the
Glenister case, both the minority and majority judgments emphasised that the constitution required effective action against
corruption, and both judgments emphasised the duty to establish effective mechanisms to combat corruption.

Section 7(2) of the constitution required the state to respect,
protect, promote and fulfil the rights in the Bill of Rights. Giv-
en that corruption infringed on the rights in the Bill of Rights,
this section required the state to prevent and combat corruption
in all its forms. In particular, it required a comprehensive response to corruption, which includes efficient anti-corruption
mechanisms.

'If the Government's constitutional duty – post Glenister – is
to create efficient anti-corruption mechanisms,' the SAIRR
heads of argument concluded, 'then that duty must similarly

inform government's conduct in response to a serious request for a commission of enquiry to be appointed into the arms deal. Where the other mechanisms – the "parallel processes" which the President invoked in his refusal – are found not to be efficient or effective, or sufficiently independent, as intended by the Court in Glenister, then it cannot be a reasonable exercise of the government's duty to refuse such a request.'

The heads of argument also responded to the Chief Justice's questions in some detail. First, the SAIRR argued that, given that the president derived all his powers – including the power to appoint commissions of inquiry – from the constitution, the Constitutional Court was empowered to scrutinise the exercise of that power, whatever the circumstances. In other words, the issue was not whether the court might scrutinise, but how, and what the outcome of that scrutiny would be. While in most matters the standard of review would be rationality, a higher form of scrutiny was required in cases involving the executive and in respect of decisions that impacted upon rights in the Bill of Rights.

The constitution did not oblige the president to appoint a commission of inquiry whenever there were indications of corruption, malfeasance and misfeasance in relation to public procurement. Where government corruption was indicated, the president was required to take reasonable steps to deal with the matter, and a judicial commission of inquiry was one of the tools in his arsenal. Thus the court had to consider whether a decision not to appoint a commission of inquiry constituted a reasonable step, in the light of the nature of the corruption indicated, and the other steps taken or available. Where the nature of the corruption would be well suited to consideration by a commission of inquiry, and no adequate other steps were taken (or were reasonably possible), the failure to appoint a commission of enquiry might be regarded as unreasonable (and irrational).

The question was ultimately whether the government had provided effective mechanisms for dealing with corruption. A commission of inquiry into corruption-related issues would be constitutionally required when no other investigative body was able or likely to conduct the necessary inquiries, or when a degree of independence was required because of the subject matter. In these situations, the court should declare the president's decision not to appoint such a judicial enquiry as unconstitutional.

'Indications of corruption, malfeasance and misfeasance in relation to public procurement oblige the appointment of a commission of inquiry when a failure to do so in the particular circumstances would not be reasonable or rational. Any attempt to prevent a full and proper inquiry into the arms deal could never be reasonable or rational.' Given this, the heads of argument suggested, the president was constitutionally obliged to appoint a commission of inquiry.

President Motlanthe's decision in December 2008 not to appoint a judicial commission of inquiry and rather to rely on 'ordinary' law enforcement when he knew the DSO was to be disbanded (which he personally authorised a few weeks later) was clearly not reasonable in the circumstances. In the light of clear inactivity by any other competent or independent body, the continued failure by presidents Motlanthe and Zuma to appoint a commission of inquiry as requested was also unreasonable.

'Given the vital importance of these issues,' the heads of argument stated, 'the Court should issue a declarator confirming that the decisions are unconstitutional, and declaring that the president is constitutionally obliged to appoint an independent judicial commission of inquiry as the only independent and effective – and hence the only reasonable and rational – means of getting to the bottom of the allegations of corruption surrounding the arms deal.'

The court need not resolve any disputes of fact before ordering the appointment of a commission of inquiry. All disputes of fact could be dealt with by the commission itself. The court could only determine whether oral evidence had to be led, and how this should be done, once the president had filed full affidavits, and the applicant had replied.

The heads of argument concluded: 'We submit that it is not appropriate for the president to state that if he were to respond to the factual allegations, disputes of fact would arise. Rather, the president should respond on affidavit, and then this Court will be the proper arbiter of whether bona fide disputes of fact have arisen, and how they should be dealt with. It is not for the president to second-guess such a consideration by this Court.'

Chapter 4

The president throws in the towel

———•———

'When someone puts an end to something, it doesn't mean that he gave up, it means that thing is not taking him anywhere.'
– Michael Bassey Johnson

THE CONSTITUTIONAL Court is a creation of the post-liberation constitution. In the old South Africa, it did not exist. In those years, South Africa had a sovereign parliament, which put white and mainly male parliamentarians at the apex of power. Now, in our constitutional democracy, this place has been taken by the constitution, which is supreme. No other law or government action can supersede the provisions of the constitution. Among other things, this means politicians can't do what they like, and the laws they pass have to comply with the constitution. No such constraints applied in the old system.

This change is one of the major differences between the old and new South Africa. In the latter, any law or conduct that is inconsistent with the constitution and the rule of law (which also has supreme status) is invalid, and liable to be struck down or corrected by the courts.

The Constitutional Court has the final say about whether contested laws or actions comply with the constitution. This is very different from the far weaker role played by courts in the apartheid era and in preceding dispensations since Union in 1910.

The Constitutional Court also differs from the Supreme Court of Appeal in that it has more than appellate jurisdiction. As noted briefly in the previous chapter, it is possible, in certain circumstances, to approach the court directly, as a court of first instance. It prefers to sit as an appellate tribunal that has the benefit of the analysis of the lower courts, but does not shirk from exercising original jurisdiction when the occasion demands this, and when it is in the interests of justice to do so.

The matter between Terry Crawford-Browne and the president was such an instance. The president's conduct in refusing to appoint a commission of inquiry into possible malfeasance or misfeasance in the arms procurement processes was under scrutiny for its compliance with the constitution and its consistency with the rule of law. A Constitutional Court hearing was not Terry's first choice. A completed trial in the Western Cape High Court would have better suited his strategy, as it would have enabled him to subpoena the financial records of the ANC in order to establish the link between bribes paid and political party funding before the trial.

This outcome did not materialise. The president's legal team prevented Terry from proceeding in the High Court by taking an exception which seemed highly arguable and would have delayed the matter for years if litigated through the High Court, the Supreme Court of Appeal and, finally, the Constitutional Court.

Following the Fred Daniel case, we now know that the Constitutional Court does not regard a disputed request for a commission of inquiry as something that falls within its exclusive jurisdiction. In the bigger scheme of things, Terry secured a hearing without the delays and expenses involved in the usual route via the High Court and the Supreme Court of Appeal due to the tactics adopted against him. However, as the Constitutional Court does not hear trials, it was not possible to subpoena documents to show the existence of bribes for the benefit of the ANC. To that extent, the president's tactics worked to the benefit of him and his political party.

The Constitutional Court is housed in a beautiful new building on Constitution Hill in Braamfontein, Johannesburg, the site of a fort, which became a notorious prison, built by Paul Kruger's government in the old Boer Republic. The entire precinct has been restored and remodelled, and the Old Fort Prison is now a museum and exhibition centre. The awaiting-trial wing was demolished, and the bricks were used to help build the court building. The court building has large street-level windows, meant to symbolise the transparent administration of justice. In practice, it means that court sessions are visible to pedestrians outside the building, and those in the courtroom can see the feet of pedestrians on the pavement outside.

The court houses an impressive art collection, and its interior is tastefully decorated. In a bow to tradition, the long curved bench where the judges sit during court sessions is covered with the hides of indigenous Nguni cattle. There is ample provision for members of the public, and the court is always as neat as a pin, with polished floors and polite staff. It has become a tourist attraction, deservedly so, and retired justices are wont to offer tours, laced with anecdotes, to those who visit it.

Thoughts of tours and anecdotes could not have been further from our minds as we prepared argument for the hearing set down for 5 May 2011. Terry flew up on the morning of the hearing to spare himself the cost of accommodation. Peter Hazell and I were given a free room each in the rectory of St Mary's Anglican Church in Rosettenville, courtesy of my sister and brother-in-law, Peta and Rod Greville. He was the priest in charge. We did not dare rely on any airlines to get us to court in time by flying on the day.

Charles Abrahams, our intrepid instructing attorney, and Terry's long-standing advisor, had other business in Johannesburg and spent the night before the hearing at a hotel in Braamfontein, near the court. We met him in good time on the morning of the hearing, and made our way to the court in a state of nervous anticipation.

The Constitutional Court always sits *en banc*. While eight justices form a quorum, all 11 often take their places on the bench. Facing this array of judicial talent is a daunting experience even for the most experienced counsel. Eleven highly intelligent people picking your arguments to pieces is frightening enough. When this happens in public, in the full glare of the media, it is terrifying. When those eleven people are the cream of the country's judges, one can only cope by going into adrenalin overdrive.

The judges are seldom hostile, and never rude. Their questions are aimed at testing the arguments put forward by the various parties. Sometimes, though, it seems as if all of them want their questions answered at the same time.

Counsel in a given matter are normally greeted by the presiding justice (usually the Chief Justice or the Deputy Chief Justice) in a lounge elsewhere in the building. Pleasantries are exchanged, and each advocate is given a certain amount of time for his or her presentation, a measure aimed at hearing matters efficiently and economically. This court is not a place for waffling; cases are largely won and lost on the heads of argument filed, and oral arguments rarely play a decisive role.

This procedure was not observed on 5 May 2011 when counsel for the president and the *amicus curiae* joined us at the court, robed and ready for action. Instead, counsel were called into the justices' boardroom, where the Chief Justice awaited us. These sorts of meetings are confidential, so I can't report on what happened. The meeting did not take long, and we all trooped back to court with a better understanding of how the matter would be heard.

After the matter had been formally called in open court, and counsel – Marumo Moerane SC for the government, Max du Plessis for the *amicus,* and I – introduced our teams, I was asked to start argument. Very soon, though, Chief Justice Sandile Ngcobo, presented us with a stark choice: we could either proceed with the application asking the court to compel the president to deal with the merits of Terry's case, or we could press on without the benefit of the president's version of events. Moerane was given a similar choice. Was he prepared to rely solely on technical defences, or respond to Terry's allegations?

We took instructions, and consulted with the team representing the SAIRR. The court's willingness to press on without a response from the respondents heartened us all, as the merits would then have to be regarded as undisputed. We decided to abandon the application to compel the filing of affidavits on the merits, and get on with our case.

Moerane wanted the hearing to be confined to technical points and to be given an opportunity to submit an affidavit concerning the merits at a later stage, should the need arise. The judges would have none of this. Moerane was in a corner and, quite rightly, did not have much confidence in his technical arguments. We were in the Constitutional Court because of the exception he had taken to a High Court hearing, and the mood of the judges seemed to indicate that they were prepared to entertain the matter in its entirety. So the president then asked for time to file affidavits dealing with the merits, something he had clearly tried to avoid up until then.

The judges were prepared to grant us a short period in which to get the papers into the order they wanted. This would involve amplifying our 'lean and mean' submissions, to which the president's team would need to respond. It was clear that the judges wanted to get to grips with the merits, and did not want to hear technical arguments first and argument on the merits later. Moerane was driven to ask for a postponement to prepare his amplified affidavits. The judges provided the parties with a new timetable, culminating in a hearing on 20 September 2011, a mere four months later.

Terry was understandably disappointed that the case had not been finalised. Our decision to abandon the application aimed at compelling the president to deal with the merits had been a gamble, aimed at getting the matter heard on the papers as they stood. This carried the risk that our 'lean and mean' papers would not contain enough to justify a conclusion that the presi-

dent's refusal to appoint a commission of inquiry was irrational or unreasonable. Issues surrounding hearsay evidence and
rumours of impropriety could be addressed by obtaining further affidavits, and shoring up Terry's case in this way.

We were out of the court building before our cars had had
time to heat up in the autumn sun. However, this damp squib
was not our first surprise. A few days later, the Chief Justice
issued directions designed to put an end to requests for further
delays. In essence, he instructed the parties to supplement their
papers by setting out the evidence relevant to the case by way
of affidavits, including affidavits from witnesses able to confirm the allegations made. We had to lodge our supplementary
papers by 15 June, and the respondents had to lodge their
response by 1 August. Following this, we had to lodge supplementary written arguments by 15 August; the *amicus curiae*, by
15 August; and the first respondent by 29 August.

We set to work immediately to beef up the bare-bones case
we had presented. This involved assembling many documents,
and taking affidavits from witnesses ranging from Andrew
Feinstein, the former ANC MP and SCOPA member, to Jonathan Shapiro, the cartoonist better known as Zapiro. His cartoons on the arms deals were critical of the government and
presidents Mbeki and Zuma in ways that could have, but did
not, provoke defamation claims.

Given the weight and scope of evidence, the president asked
for more time to deal with the allegations. Accordingly, on
15 August, the court issued new directions, to the effect that
the hearing had been moved from 20 September to 17 November. Now, our supplementary papers had to be lodged by 15 June

and the respondents' response by 15 September 2011. We had to lodge our supplementary written argument by 29 September; the *amicus curiae* by 29 September; and the first respondent by 13 October.

My heart sank as I read these dates. It meant I would receive a huge pile of paper on 15 September, the date of my wedding anniversary, and the president's supplementary argument on my birthday. I hoped the response to the supplemented founding papers would arrive late on 15 September, so that I could still enjoy the anniversary. We duly submitted our supplementary papers; it was clear that a gargantuan task awaited anyone wishing to dispute Terry's allegations.

The big day, 15 September, dawned bright and clear. My wife, Elise, and I decided to celebrate early, in the certain knowledge that a lot of work would start later. I switched off my phone, and we lunched at a posh hotel with a good view of the sea. Imagine my surprise when I turned on the phone an hour or so later and found 44 new messages. While we were lunching, the president had thrown in the towel. He had announced a decision to appoint a commission of inquiry, and would file no opposing papers beyond a short affidavit.

In essence, it said he did not concede that declining to appoint a commission of inquiry into the arms deal was unconstitutional. However, because the litigation had started so along ago, and there were 'several developments' since then with a bearing on his decision, he had decided to appoint a commission. Its terms of reference, composition and time frame would be announced later. Given this, there was no longer any dispute between the applicant and the respondents that required the determination of the Constitutional Court. In order to finalise the matter, the respondents would carry the costs of the application thus far.

The rest of the wedding anniversary celebrations were far more exuberant. The first journalist to get hold of me was Paul Kirk, then working for *The Citizen* in KwaZulu-Natal. His call came through as I was trawling through the 44 messages, most of them from other reporters. When he told me about the announcement, I asked him not to crack jokes about such a serious matter. But he insisted that the announcement appeared to be genuine. It began to dawn on me why there were so many messages on my phone. The impossible had happened – Terry would get the inquiry, and we had done it without proving irrationality in court.

The president had new advisors in the matter, led by Nazier Cassim SC of the Johannesburg Bar. Cassim phoned me, and we tidied up loose ends about costs. In the light of the president's volte face, they even agreed to pay the costs of the *amicus curiae*.

It's not entirely clear why they changed their minds. Perhaps the president wanted to retain control of the situation, and feared that the court might impose onerous conditions on him. Perhaps he had accepted advice that his prospects of success were not good. We will never know, and don't really need to know. He had thrown in the towel, and that was all that mattered for the moment.

In a final effort, Terry asked the court to rule that retired rather than sitting judges should be appointed to the commission, on the grounds that it would be easier to compromise sitting judges who were eager for promotion by the executive branch of government, or create the impression that they had been compromised. The same suspicion of bias is less likely to arise in the case of a retired judge, who would no longer harbour such ambitions. While this made eminent sense in practical terms, it was a bit of a stretch in legal terms, and the president's attorney objected in an affidavit that accurately set out the relevant points of law. It was our turn to throw in the towel; we did not press the point, and the matter was dealt with by consent when it was called in open court on 17 November, just over a year after our first approach to the Constitutional Court. Only one advocate representing the president appeared in court, to note the withdrawal of the application and the agreement in respect of costs.

In this way, the long-awaited Seriti Commission, or Arms Procurement Commission of Inquiry, came into being, exactly three years after the Social Justice Coalition had begun its campaign.

Chapter 5

The Seriti whitewash

———◆———

*'One who retreats to fight another day isn't running
away, but looking for another road towards the
same destination.'*

– Lionel Suggs

IN THE spring of 2011, the then minister of justice, Jeff Radebe,
duly instructed by President Zuma, sprang to work to appoint
the commission of inquiry into the arms procurement agreements of 1999.

There was a lot of speculation about its terms of reference.
Would the government try to cripple the probe, or give the commissioners a broad enough mandate to get to the truth? Who
would the commissioners be – independent thinkers, or government 'yes-men' who would simply perpetuate the arms
deal cover-up? This deception had started in the national
executive, continued in parliament shortly after the deals had
been concluded, and persisted over the years, to the chagrin
of activists and opposition politicians, the bemusement of the
general public, and pacifists' fury.

Given that the arms deals – the biggest set of public procurements in South African history – were financed with taxpayers'
money, they were, and remain, an issue of public interest. A responsive and accountable government should not allow bribery

and other irregularities in the course of public procurement, and evidence of bribery and corruption should not be concealed from the public. The notion of a constitutional democracy under the rule of law does not align with an avaricious elite using the levers of power to its own advantage instead of in the public interest.

In the event, the arms deal cover-up ended or crippled several political careers. Andrew Feinstein, an ANC MP and leader of its SCOPA team, was the first victim. (SCOPA is the parliamentary Standing Committee on Public Accounts, which interrogates government expenditure on behalf of the voting public, and is usually chaired by a member of the opposition). Feinstein wanted SCOPA to hold the executive to account for the arms procurement process. The ANC top brass did not. Feinstein quickly found himself in the political wilderness, resigned from parliament, and took a job in London, where he now lives.

Raenette Taljaard, a DA MP and the youngest member of the first democratic parliament, tried valiantly to get answers to her party's questions about the arms deals. She failed, resigned from parliament, and became executive director of the HSF. She also served part-time on the Independent Electoral Commission, but resigned in the wake of a procurement scandal in which she was not implicated. She now teaches public policy at the University of Cape Town.

The arms deal also ended the parliamentary career of ANC stalwart Tony Yengeni. In 1998, it emerged that he had bought a luxury Mercedes-Benz sports utility vehicle at a heavily discounted price from a company involved in the arms deals, and had not declared this benefit to parliament. All this happened while he was serving as the chairman of the parliamentary standing committee on defence, which was overseeing the arms procurement process. Once the story broke, wags dubbed the model of vehicle in question a 'Yengeni'.

As a result, Yengeni – who by then was serving as the ANC's parliamentary chief whip – was charged with fraud and corruption. After fighting the charges tooth and nail, he eventually entered into a plea bargain – negotiated with the then minister of justice, Dr Penuell Maduna, and national director of public prosecutions, Bulelane Ngcuka, at a meeting at the minister's home. In terms of the plea bargain, the charges of corruption were dropped in favour of a lesser charge of defrauding parliament. Some wondered whether this bargain was struck in order to avoid further exposure of corruption in the course of the arms deals.

Yengeni stoutly contended that the plea bargain included an agreement that he would not have to go to jail. The prosecution denied this, and Yengeni was sentenced to four years imprisonment. Following a series of failed appeals, he eventually went to jail, but was released on parole just five months later. Leading members of the ANC carried him shoulder-high to prison, and greeted his release in similar style. Following his conviction, he resigned from parliament, but continued to serve on the ANC's national executive committee.

In August 2015, Thandi Modise, then chairperson of the National Council of Provinces, declared that parliament had 'let Yengeni down' by disciplining him for his breach of parliamentary ethics without explaining the serious nature of the situation to him. Whether this astonishing statement was another attempt to airbrush the arms deals malfeasance out of history or simply a symptom of the general loss of moral compass among government leaders is a matter of opinion.

Besides Yengeni's incarceration, the only other person who served time for corruption in relation to the arms deals was Schabir Shaik, former financial adviser to President Zuma. From 2004 to 2005, Shaik was tried in the KwaZulu-Natal High Court in a long trial presided over by acting justice Hilary Squires, a veteran of service in Zimbabwe's beleaguered judiciary.

One of the charges in that case related to the payment of 'protection money' by a South African company called Thint – a joint venture between Shaik and a French arms manufacturer aimed at profiting from the South African arms deals – to none other than Jacob Zuma. This charge, and many others, were proven beyond a reasonable doubt to the satisfaction of the trial court, the Supreme Court of Appeal, and the Constitutional Court. Shaik was sentenced to 15 years in prison. In March 2009, after serving two years and four months of his sentence, Shaik was released on medical parole, which is usually only extended to prisoners who are terminally ill. After his release, Shaik's health improved markedly, to the extent that he was photographed on the golf courses of Durban, and smoking fat cigars. In 2015 he asked, without success, for his medical parole conditions to be relaxed as he found them 'burdensome'.

Following Shaik's conviction, Zuma resigned from parliament, and was dismissed as deputy president by then President Thabo Mbeki. Shaik's successful prosecution emboldened the NPA to reconsider the opinion of its former national director, Bulelani Ngcuka, in the matter. On 24 July 2003, Ngcuka told black editors, famously so, of leading newspapers that while there was a prima facie case of corruption against Zuma, he was not prepared to charge him, as the case was not winnable. But the outcome of the Shaik case provided cause for reflection. Shaik's generally corrupt relationship with Zuma had been proven; if the corruptee, Zuma, had the same intention, matching that of Shaik, he could be successfully charged with corruption as well.

The new head of the NPA, Vusi Pikoli, reviewed the matter, and decided to proceed with Zuma's prosecution. This cost Pikoli his job. In September 2007, he was suspended for seeking to prosecute Jackie Selebi, the national commissioner of police, on charges of corruption, and in February 2008, by which time Zuma was president of the ANC, parliament decided to dismiss him. Fancy excuses for doing so were cooked up, but the simple truth is that he was dismissed for deciding to proceed with prosecuting Zuma. Selebi's prosecution succeeded, thanks to good investigative work by the Scorpions. Years later, via Facebook, then ex-president Mbeki sought to justify his decision to suspend Pikoli on the basis that he had feared open warfare between the police and the Scorpions.

In April 2009, Pikoli's acting successor, the more malleable Mokotedi Mpshe, decided that Zuma's prosecution, which he had initiated in December 2007, should not proceed as this matter had been 'irreparably polluted' by political interference in the prosecution process. The DA promptly took this decision on legal review on the grounds of irrationality. In April 2016, the full bench of the North Gauteng High Court found in its favour. In late 2016, when this book went to press, the appeal processes were still pending, and it seemed likely – given the appeal processes available to the losing party, probably Zuma – that it would still take some time to conclude. If the review succeeds, Zuma will face 783 charges of corruption, fraud, money laundering and racketeering, some related to the arms deals.

On 13 May 2016, James Selfe, chairperson of the DA's Federal Executive, explained this matter to members of the media and others at the Cape Town Press Club. I reproduce his address in full, partly because of the way in which it unravels the intricacies of this case, and partly because it illustrates the tenacity required to pursue these sorts of issues in the face of determined political resistance drawing on effectively unlimited state resources – in this instance, almost R50 million of taxpayers' money.

> On 29 April [2016], the North Gauteng High Court granted our application to review and set aside the decision by the then Acting National Director of Public Prosecutions, taken (appropriately) on 1 April 2009, to discontinue the prosecution against Jacob Zuma. Until then, this prosecution had been described as the best prepared criminal prosecution in South African legal history.
>
> This application was resisted with great determination and about R49 million of your and my money, over the last seven years.
>
> A review application usually starts with a request, in terms of Rule 53 of the Uniform Rules of Court, to provide the 'record of decision', that is, all the material that was

before the decision-maker when he or she took the impugned decision. In this particular case, the record included the intercepted conversations between Bulelani Ngcuka and Leonard McCarthy, which had been cited as the reason why Adv Mpshe had discontinued the prosecution. It is for this reason that this litigation became known as the 'spy tapes' case.

The proceedings started in the North Gauteng High Court in June 2010. The NPA raised two interlocutory applications, first, that the DA did not have standing to bring the application, and secondly, that a decision to discontinue a prosecution was not reviewable. In the circumstances, it said that it was not obliged to hand over the spy tapes. The Court agreed.

We took the matter on appeal to the Supreme Court of Appeal, which ruled in our favour in March 2012, and found that the DA did have locus standi and that a decision to discontinue the prosecution was reviewable. It ordered the NPA to hand over the record within 14 days.

The NPA stubbornly refused to do so, citing that Mr Zuma's representations, which formed part of the record, were privileged, and therefore could not be released without his permission, which he naturally refused.

In August 2013, we brought an application for an order to compel the NPA to hand over the record. We won the case, but Mr Zuma appealed it. We had to return to the SCA, where we obtained an order that compelled the NPA to hand over a redacted record. That record was handed over to us in October 2014, and we could begin the preparations for the substantive review, which, after extensive delays, was set down for hearing at the beginning of March this year.

As you all know, the Court found that the decision to

discontinue the prosecution was irrational, and set it aside. In the words of the judgment: 'Mr Zuma should face the charges as outlined in the indictment.' We now have that judgment, and the question is: where to from here?

Mr Zuma and the NPA obviously have the right to appeal this judgment, and if that right is exercised, it must be exercised by close of business on Monday 23 May. If they do so, they will have two paths: first, they can apply to the North Gauteng High Court for leave to appeal. The test for a successful application for appeal is that another court could come to a different conclusion. The problem for Zuma and the NPA is that this judgment was a unanimous decision of a full bench headed up by the Deputy Judge President. It is difficult to conceive that those judges would believe that another court would come to different conclusion.

If the High Court refuses an application for leave to appeal, Zuma and the NPA can petition the Supreme Court of Appeal for leave to appeal. That court may entertain an appeal, but I cannot see it coming to a different conclusion. I suppose an application for direct access to appeal to the Constitutional Court is also possible, but is very rarely granted, and I doubt that it would succeed.

Mr Zuma could also consider an application for a permanent stay of prosecution. He was preparing one in 2009, and I imagine this could be reintroduced. Again, the mountain that he would have to climb would be to persuade a court that a case that was so well prepared ought summarily to be abandoned. Unless there is compelling evidence that some other aspect of the prosecution that is defective, most courts would say that the trial should proceed, and that the trial court can decide if the case is defective.

This is also what the NPA's answer was (at least initially) to Michael Hulley following the representations that were made to drop the charges back in 2009.

In addition, Adv Abrahams, the new national director of public prosecutions, could decide, like Adv Mpshe, to drop the charges. He might argue that, after all the time that has elapsed, the chances of a successful prosecution have diminished. This court judgment, however, has established that such a decision has to be rational and that it is reviewable. Accordingly, we would naturally look very closely at Adv Abrahams's reasons, and we would have no hesitation in taking this decision, too, on review if the decision appeared to be irrational.

Adv Mpshe relied, when he took the 2009 decision, on the concept of abuse of process. This related to the intercepted conversations between Ngcuka and McCarthy relating to whether the indictment should be served before, during or after the Polokwane Conference. This was, without doubt, reprehensible conduct, and McCarthy should have been disciplined, if not prosecuted. But the alleged abuse of purpose did not concern the inherent merits of the prosecution case.

It had only to do with the timing of the service of the indictment, and in the end, the serving of the indictment made no difference at all to the outcome of the Polokwane conference. In addition, even if there had been an abuse of process, the Pretoria High Court found very clearly that the place to determine whether there had been an abuse would likewise be the trial court.

It would seem, then, that the trial should go ahead, and that Adv Abrahams ought to refer the docket to a court, and set a trial date. I suppose that, if one really wanted to, one could ensure that the prosecution did not succeed by under-resourcing the prosecution, or prosecuting in a half-hearted way – let's say, by assigning the assistant prosecutor in the traffic court to this case. That was the strategy recently adopted by the SABC when the DA obtained a judgment from the SCA that the Public Protector's remedial action, which included ordering that Hlaudi Motsoeneng face a disciplinary enquiry, were legally enforceable. The SABC then convened a sham disciplinary enquiry, which predictably exonerated Mr Motsoeneng. We are taking this matter on review as well.

So the saga is by no means over. People often ask me whether it's worth the trouble, the expense, and the tension that this creates between the judiciary and the executive. My answer is an unequivocal yes. This, and a number of other cases, have established a number of very important principles, of which the most important is that no one, however powerful, well-connected or well-resourced is above the law. And that's well worth fighting for.

But back to our main story. Zuma did not seem troubled by any implicit conflicts of interest when, in October 2011, he announced the commission of inquiry into the arms procurement process. Initially, three commissioners were appointed. The first was Willie Seriti, an Appeal Court judge and former Pretoria attorney. The second was Willem van der Merwe, the Gauteng judge who had acquitted Zuma in his infamous rape case in which he had earned his shower-head in Zapiro cartoons. This adornment is a reference to Zuma's explanation that while he knew the complainant was HIV-positive, he took a shower after 'consensual sex' with her to prevent becoming infected himself. The third commissioner was Francis Legodi, a Gauteng judge, and very much his own man. Van der Merwe declined the appointment 'for personal reasons', and was replaced by the retiring judge-president of the Free State, Thekiso Musi.

The terms of reference of the Commission of Inquiry into Allegations of Fraud, Corruption, Impropriety or Irregularity in the Strategic Defence Procurement Package (SDPP) were gazetted in October 2011. The commission would investigate:

- the rationale for the SDPP;
- whether the arms and equipment acquired in terms of the SDPP were being underutilised, or not utilised at all;
- whether the offsets and job opportunities meant to flow from the SDPP had materialised, and if not, what should be done to realise them;
- whether anyone within and outside South Africa had improperly influenced any of the contracts, and if so, whether legal steps should be taken against them;
- whether any such people could be sued for any losses that the state might have suffered as a result of their conduct; and
- whether any contract was tainted by fraud or corruption which could be proven to the extent that this would justify its cancellation.

The commission was instructed to complete its work within two years, and hand its final report to the president within six months thereafter. Regulations would be made later to enable the Commission to conduct its work meaningfully and effectively, and to facilitate the gathering of evidence by conferring on the

Commission 'powers such as are necessary, including the power to enter and search premises, secure the attendance of witnesses and compel the production of documents'.

Vas Soni SC of the Johannesburg Bar was appointed as chief evidence leader. I wrote to him to congratulate him and to give him the benefit of a few insights I had gathered along the way. This is what I wrote:

Dear Vas

Congratulations on your appointment as chief evidence leader in the Seriti Commission of Inquiry into wrong-doing in the procurement of armaments for the new South Africa. This is indubitably the brief of your life, and a golden opportunity to assist the Commission with its task of exacting accountability in respect of all matters covered by the broad mandate which the president has given it.

In your capacity as the senior evidence leader, you will be in a position to help and guide the commissioners in their search for the truth behind the allegations which have bedevilled the arms deals virtually since the day when they were concluded. It is self-evident that the approach which you adopt in discharging your obligations towards the public, the Commission and the president should be open, transparent and accountable.

At this stage, you are probably wondering where to start on an intercontinental journey which is likely to take you the full two years which the president has allowed and which will undoubtedly involve you in the perusal of numerous documents and the taking of many state-ments. There is already a great deal of information in the public domain which you and your team are going to have to sift for the Commission in a manner which is relevant and digestible to the commissioners, as well as being conducive to the discharge of their mandate. Five books which touch upon, or are devoted to, the subject of the arms deals have already been published. There are doubtless more to come.

The books already published, in order of their publication, are: *Eye on the Money*, by Terry Crawford-Browne; *After the Party,* by Andrew Feinstein (now in its second edition); *The Arms Deal in Your Pocket*, by Paul Holden (which has a most useful timeline as its Appendix B); *The Devil in the Detail*, by Paul Holden and Hennie van Vuuren; and *The Shadow World – Inside the Global Arms Trade*, by Andrew Feinstein.

It would seem that all of these books are required reading for the Commission, and that the authors may be used as witnesses in respect of the specific issues which are covered by the terms of reference of the Commission. All of the authors have indicated their willingness to participate in the activities of the Commission, and their knowledge of the facts and acquired expertise in relation to the issues which the Commission will be investigating could prove to be invaluable to you and your fellow evidence leaders.

There is also the record of the proceedings in the Constitutional Court in which Terry Crawford-Browne sought an order compelling the appointment of the Commission of Inquiry. His supplementary affidavit and that of Richard Young are a veritable treasure trove of information that will be of interest to the Commission. Richard Young has already successfully litigated a damages claim against the government because his company was a victim of the wrongful manner in which the procurement process was conducted.

There is also other litigation on record in the High Court which will be of interest to you. In particular, the last gasp effort of the Scorpions to bring wrongdoers in the BAe/Saab deal to book contains details of the modus operandi used to launder bribes through the British Virgin Islands banking system, with interesting details of amounts and recipients all on record already. These few pages could render it unnecessary for the Commission to plough through the millions of pages of documents in the possession of the Hawks. There are three pending criminal investigations in the hands of the Hawks, and the content of the dockets in those matters will be of considerable interest to the Commission. The court file relating to the freezing of some of the assets of Fana Hlongwana also makes instructive reading.

You will also have to take cognisance of the criminal investigations and various admissions made in the countries in which the arms manufacturers who did the arms deals are resident. The Swedish authorities have a docket open against Saab, and there are criminal investigations still pending in Germany. The details of these are known to Mr Crawford-Browne who visited Germany in March 2011 to consult with prosecutors there as part of the preparation of his own case. It seems that the Serious Fraud Office in the United Kingdom, while it no longer has open dockets, will be a source of much useful information.

One of the matters that will engage your attention at the outset is the order in which to tackle the work of the Commission. In this regard, you may wish to consider the 'low-hanging fruit' that is available to you as a consequence of admissions made in relation to the aircraft and submarine deals. As long ago as 2003, an admission was made in the British House of Commons that the 'commissions' (for which read 'bribes') paid in the BAe/Saab arms deal had been kept 'within reasonable limits' (sic) because £200 million had been set aside for this purpose, and only £114 million was used. This, coupled with the recent admissions by Saab, ought, at common law, to afford a basis for cancelling what was the biggest of the four arms deals. The British Virgin Islands banking records show a paper trail of the destination of the bribes admittedly paid by BAe/Saab.

The other matter which may be solved easily is the submarine deal in which the new management of Ferrostaal has made public an attorney's report reflecting details of the wrongdoing in the acquisition of submarines by South Africa. This has been done in an effort to prove to American authorities that Ferrostaal has turned over a new leaf, and that is worthy of tendering for large US contracts.

If the first interim report of the Commission concentrates on the jet and submarine deals, it will be possible to reflect a great deal of constructive progress in a short time. This will have the effect of establishing public confidence in the work of the Commission, and will enable the Executive to give its consideration to cancelling the jet and submarine deals. South Africa can reclaim all payments made, be excused from liability in respect of payments not yet due, against return of the jets and submarines to the suppliers. The beauty of cancelling is that bribes paid are recoverable from the bribers, as they were paid out of the prices agreed.

The other deals will not be as easy to crack, but Bell Helicopters has publicly complained that it was asked for bribes in regard to the helicopter contract, while a careful interview with Barbara Masekela, our former ambassador to Paris, may reveal interesting information concerning the propriety of the warships deal.

It is also important that you keep an open line of communication with the public by way of regular press releases, the establishment of a Commission website, and maybe even a Facebook page. Possible whistle blowers should be given the opportunity of communicating with you anonymously and electronically via the website using internet cafés. In this way, identities can be protected and valuable information can be obtained with the minimum of effort on the part of your evidence leading team. The two years available to you to discharge your work suggests that you will have to keep the exhortation of section 237 of the Constitution uppermost in your mind by performing diligently and without delay. You have an awesome responsibility as evidence leader and deserve the co-operation and assistance of the public, those who investigated wrongdoing, both locally and overseas, and the apparatus of the State. Look up surviving Scorpions investigators and prosecutors, especially those who looked so forlorn when the 783 charges against the president were dropped. Good luck!

Paul Hoffman SC
14 November 2011

Unfortunately, it emerged that Soni was subject to a conflict of interest because he had previously done some legal work for one of the arms dealers. He did give my letter to the commission, and I was contacted about it years later, but Soni did not even start his work. He was replaced by the affable Tayob 'Pops' Aboobaker SC of the Durban Bar.

The Seriti Commission started off slowly, and was soon mired in controversy. The worst of Terry's fears expressed in the affidavits to the Constitutional Court about the wisdom of appointing sitting judges to investigate such a politically loaded and controversial topic seemed to be realised. One of the commissioners, Judge Francis Legodi, soon resigned 'for personal reasons', as did Aboobaker. This was preceded by the resignation of the senior investigator Norman Moabi.

In his letter of resignation, dated 7 January 2013, which he made public, Moabi declared he was resigning because there were two agendas at work within the commission: 'one as defined in the terms of reference, and the other, the real work in progress at the Commission that will deliver the report to the President of the RSA'.

The second agenda was marked by 'obsessive' control of the flow of information by the chairperson; clandestine preparations of documents and/or briefs handed to the evidence leaders; unknown person(s) dictating which information should go into the briefs, which evidence leaders would deal with which witnesses, and why; unknown criteria used to determine which professionals/attorneys were to be paired to specific evidence leaders, and why; strict instructions to evidence leaders to contact only one person in respect of any queries; and professional staff having no knowledge of the contents of files sent to evidence leaders.

Input from any individuals within the commission who did not advance this second agenda was excluded, and professional staff were 'deliberately distracted' by keeping them occupied with matters that would not ultimately form part of the brief.

Comments by key figures within the commission supporting the existence of a hidden agenda, the letter stated, included the following: 'When we will have dealt with the first witnesses, they will not again make noises in the public media'; and 'When you look at the submissions made by the Terry Crawford Browns (sic) of this world, you realise that they are not factual but are based on hearsay. There is no substance in what they have said in the public media up to now.'

Early on in its activities, Terry asked me to write to the commission, recording his alarm at the direction it was taking. This is what I wrote in February 2013, and after the letter went unanswered, I released it in the public interest.

The importance of getting it right in the Arms Procurement Commission

The late Mr Justice Arthur Chaskalson, then President of the Constitutional Court, later Chief Justice of South Africa, in a paper delivered at the Annual General Meeting of the Law Society of Transvaal on Friday 28 October 1994 in Pretoria, said: 'We need to remember that the first incursion into rights is often the most damaging; that once inroads are permitted, the will to resist subsequent incursions is lessened, and the ability to regain what has been lost is often extremely difficult.'

Just a few years later, after the 'first incursion' had been made, Idasa described the arms deals scandal as the 'litmus test of South Africa's commitment to democracy and good governance'. In the run-up to the long-awaited first sittings of the Arms Procurement Commission (APC), the observations quoted above come into sharp focus as the fear of failing the 'litmus test' grips the hearts of those who value freedom. Cynical observers claim that the APC is not supposed to uncover the truth, given the levels of corruption in high places. They are effectively conceding that 'what has been lost' cannot be regained. But it does not have to be so.

The APC has been rocked by the resignation of one of its senior investigators, and the public might now reasonably be apprehensive that Judge Willie Seriti is biased against those who have complained about the corruption in the arms deals. The judge could do a lot to restore confidence in the APC by answering the as yet unanswered questions which the resignation and his responses to it have raised. He has not responded positively to an invitation to do so last week. In the hope that he can be persuaded to reconsider his stance, here are some of the important questions that would have been raised had the opportunity to do so face to face been allowed:

1. Do you have any relatives, whether by blood or by marriage, on the staff and payroll of the APC? If so, is this compliant with the values and principles of section 195 of the Constitution?
2. Have you read the record in the case between Terry Crawford-Browne and the President which led to the appointment of the APC, the seven books written on the subject of wrongdoing in the arms deals, and the Debevoise & Plimpton report on corruption at Ferrostaal? If so, why do you admit that you may have said there is 'no substance' in the complaints of wrongdoing when these sources are replete with solid evidence of wrongdoing? If you have not so read, why not?
3. Did you sign the warrant authorising the making of what are now known as the 'spy tapes' that led to the 783 charges of corruption against the President being dropped? If so, was it proper for you to accept appointment to the APC, given the findings you had to make to authorise the warrant?

4. Is the Head of Research at the APC, Advocate Fanyana Mdumbe, a loyal cadre of the ANC, and a senior member of the staff of the Department of Justice? If so (and in either event), is it not an intractable conflict of interest situation that you have placed him at the APC given that his Minister was in the cabinet that allowed the conclusion of the arms deals, and is therefore collectively responsible?

5. Why have you elected to call 'complainant' witnesses first, given the bad experience of the 1990 Harms Commission which did this?

6. Is it the intention of the APC to take the evidence of the cabinet ministers and civil servants who actually negotiated the arms deals, those identified as taking bribes, those who acted as unauthorised middlemen, the arms manufacturers' representatives, and the foreign politicians whose lobbying lubricated the arms deals?

7. Why did you decline to summons Tony Blair when he was in the country?

8. Given the decision in Sparks versus The State, do you think that it is legally permissible to deal with witnesses in a way that 'they will not again make noises in the public media'? If not, why did you say (or may you have said) this, and what exactly did you mean by it?

9. What motivated you to exaggerate the 'inundation' of the APC with correspondence from Terry Crawford-Browne when he quite legitimately sent only eight emails in 2012?

10. Are the APC evidence leaders kept in separate 'silos' by you and Mdumbe? If so, why?

11. For what reasons were advocates Soni SC and Mdladla SC dismissed by the APC?

12. Please deal fully and accountably on a point-by-point

basis with all of the allegations made by Attorney Moabi in his resignation letter and the follow-up correspondence so as to restore public confidence in your probity and suitability to chair the APC.

13. What is your response to the editorials of various newspapers, already drawn to your attention, on the impact of the resignation of Moabi on your credibility, and how do you react to the opinion pieces published under the names of Judith February, Moshoeshoe Monare, Ivor Powell, Allister Sparks and twice by Paul Hoffman SC? Feel free to deal with the points raised by those who have commented online on each of the editorials and the opinion pieces listed.

A properly conducted APC presents the nation with the opportunity to rid itself of a debilitating millstone. So much energy has been expended on covering up the wrongdoing in the arms deals that there is very little capacity left for more worthy pursuits aimed at addressing the challenges of poverty, inequality, joblessness as well as the lack of proper education, health care and housing for the 12 million people in South Africa who go hungry every day. It may be too late to incarcerate the wrongdoers in the arms deals, because it is too difficult to mount a fair trial at this stage, but it is not too late to cancel the deals, return the virtually useless armaments to the manufacturers who sold them, and recover the prices paid as well as damages which may have been sustained.

An injection of R70 billion into the public purse is not to be sneezed at in these times of financial crisis. A lot of good can be done if the monies recovered are sensibly applied to addressing the challenges listed above. It is not legally necessary to go after the bribe-takers to achieve

this result, as the bribes were paid by the arms manufacturers, who are few in number and still well-heeled. They
have no legal leg to stand on if they try to recover the
bribes they paid. Dirty dogs get no dinner from the courts,
because a good cause of action cannot be founded in a
moral swamp. As Lord Denning famously put it: 'Fraud
unravels everything.'

In all these circumstances, it is to be hoped that Judge
Seriti will see his way clear to giving a full and public
response to the questions posed above. He has the opportunity to allay the reasonable apprehensions that his
handling of the resignation of Moabi have created. If he
does not want to do so, he knows what the right thing to
do is and he should do it without delay.

This (admittedly long) letter also did not elicit a response; instead, the commission retreated into silence, thereby confirming
the worst suspicions about its intentions. This response left Terry
in something of a dilemma. How was he to cope with the hos-
tility of Seriti, who controlled the commission's administration?
We formulated the following ten options:

- **Concourt deluxe option**: Ask the Constitutional Court to set
  aside the appointment of the APC after it refuses to issue
  summons against the ANC to produce its books, and direct
  Jacob Zuma to appoint retired judges in its place to perform
  its mandate. Join four arms dealers in asking for the cancellation of the deals because of already proven infringements.
  Ask for the conduct of advocates in the matter to be referred
  to the General Council of the Bar of SA, attorneys to the Law
  Society of SA, and judges to the Judicial Services Commission

(JSC). Alternatively, ask for the matter, or aspects over which the Constitutional Court does not have sole jurisdiction, to be referred to a full bench of the North Gauteng High Court.

- **Concourt standard option**: As above, without arms dealers and disciplinary steps.
- **High Court deluxe option**: Going after Seriti for his recalcitrance, and the APC for the non-issue of the ANC summons.
- **High Court standard option**: As above, without Seriti relief but say that a complaint of maladministration about his conduct has been submitted to the Office of the Public Protector.
- **JSC option**: Complain to the JSC about Seriti's conduct.
- **OPP option**: Complain to the Public Protector, Thuli Madonsela, about the maladministration of the APC.
- **Zuma option**: Letter of demand requiring the firing of the APC and its replacement with retired judges.
- **APC option**: Letter of demand requiring leave for Terry to issue his own ANC summons.
- **Go-public option**: Talk to the *Sunday Times*.
- **Walk-away option**: Give up as an act of self-preservation, and accept that ours is an irredeemably corrupt society.

Eventually, Terry took the last option, but co-operated to the extent that he gave evidence to the commission, and backed it up with a written submission. He did so out of a sense of duty rather than because he believed it would have any effect. Small wonder, then, that the commission continued to shed personnel with alarming regularity. Eventually even the evidence leaders assigned to Terry, Barry Skinner SC and his junior Carole Sibiya, both of the Durban Bar, also threw in the towel.

Terry described the activities of the commission as a farce even before he gave his evidence. Feinstein, Van Vuuren and Holden refused to give evidence because of the pusillanimous attitude of the commission to what it called 'hearsay evidence' in their books on the arms deals.

Eventually, in mid-2015, the evidence that the commission was prepared to take from state functionaries involved in the deals and from complainants had all been led, and final submissions had been made. Accountability Now made a submission on the admissibility of hearsay in a last-ditch effort to persuade the commission that its approach to unnecessarily excluding evidence was not in keeping with the role of a fact-finding entity. We did not expect this effort to succeed, but did so to smooth the way for those who might wish to take the commission on review for excluding a large volume of valuable evidence from its consideration of the matter.

The commission handed its report to President Zuma in December 2015. On 21 April 2016, Zuma released the full report – running to 767 pages in three volumes – as well as the government's response. Working its way through the terms of reference from the top down, the statement summarised the findings – reasonably accurately – as follows:

- It was necessary for the South African National Defence Force to acquire the equipment in order to carry out its constitutional mandate and international obligations of peace support and peace-keeping.
- All the arms and equipment acquired were well-utilised, and the projected number of jobs had been achieved. Anticipated

offsets had substantially materialised. Adequate arrangements were in place to ensure that those who had not met their obligations did so in the immediate future.

- Undue or improper influence had played no role in the selection of the preferred bidders. Evidence also did not support or corroborate allegations of bribery, corruption and fraud.

The Commission had probed the engagement of consultants by some of the bidding companies. Large payments made to consultants gave an impression that the money might have been destined to decision-makers in the arms procurement process, and that they might have been bribed. The fact that some of the consultants knew or had personal contact with some of the senior politicians in the government of the day had been cited as corroboration.

On this point, the Commission had stated that 'not a single iota of evidence' was placed before it showing that any of the money received by any of the consultants was paid to any officials involved in the arms deal, let alone any of the members of the inter-ministerial committee that oversaw the process, or any member of the cabinet that took the final decisions, nor was there any circumstantial evidence pointing to this.

Preferred bidders had confirmed that the money was 'for the consultants' services and nothing else'. Some of the individuals implicated in the allegations of wrongdoing gave evidence before the commission, and refuted the allegations and insinuation levelled against them. None of them was discredited as a witness.

Members of the inter-ministerial committee had refuted any

suggestions that they might have been bribed or unduly influenced in any way whatsoever. None of them was discredited as a witness.

Key members of the technical teams that conducted the extensive evaluations of all the offers refuted any suggestion that they might have been unduly influenced or in any way manipulated to produce the relevant scores or rankings. None of them was discredited as a witness, nor was any credible evidence placed before the Commission to refute their testimony.

Other than the Lead-in Fighter Trainer (LIFT) programme, the inter-ministerial committee had accepted the results of the evaluations produced by the technical teams, and recommended the preferred bidders to the cabinet.

Where the cabinet had taken a different decision, for example by selecting the BAe Hawk aircraft for the LIFT programme, it had given full reasons for this strategic decision. There was no evidence that it was tainted by any improper motives or 'criminal shenanigans', and no basis for disbelieving the evidence submitted by members of the inter-ministerial committee in this regard.

The commission had concluded by stating that there was no room for it to draw adverse inferences, inconsistent with the direct, credible evidence presented to it, in respect of all material aspects of the terms of reference.

Zuma's statement baldly concluded: 'Government has been of the view that any findings pointing to wrongdoing should be given to law enforcement agencies for further action. There are no such findings, and the Commission does not make any recommendations.' Zuma then went on to thank the commissioners for their 'professional, efficient and effective' work.

And that, as far as the president was concerned, was it. Some R137 million and five years later, the matter was done and dusted in two sentences.

The report, and the government's response, provoked a storm of protest, usefully collated by DefenceWeb. It quoted Patricia de Lille, the original whistle-blower, as saying the Seriti Commission was a 'farce' that had wasted taxpayers' money to shield the president against corruption allegations.

David Maynier, previous DA shadow minister for defence who had testified before the commission, said the report was a 'massive disappointment' that had effectively let those implicated in corruption off the hook.

Dennis Bloem of the Congress of the People (COPE) said the party was dismayed that the commission had uncovered nothing of any importance over four years of sitting. He added it was hard to understand why the commission's life had been extended from two to four years when 'not even an iota of wrongdoing was uncovered'.

Pieter Groenewald, defence spokesperson for the Freedom Front Plus (FF+), said the findings that nothing irregular had taken place, that all requirements had been met and the equipment acquired was being properly utilised was 'just not true'. Among other things, about 20 Gripens were in storage. If there were no irregularities, one had to ask why Shaik and Yengeni were found guilty for irregularities related to the arms deal, and sent to jail.

The Right2Know campaign (R2K) said it had long been clear that the commission was unwilling to fully pursue the truth, but it was shocked by the extent of the cover-up. This despite a mountain of evidence which could have helped the commission to prove wrongdoing, and findings in other courts against people who had benefited from the arms deals, including Shaik and Yengeni. It added: 'The deal involves a powerful network of people that stretches all the way to the Union Buildings.'

Terry Crawford-Browne criticised the commission's failure to investigate 4.7 million computer pages and 460 boxes of evidence against BAe that the Hawks had inherited from the Scorpions; 160 pages of affidavits from the British Serious Fraud Office and the Scorpions which detailed how and why BAe and its front company Red Diamond Trading had paid bribes of £115 million to secure the South African arms deal; and the Debevoise & Plimpton report on MAN Ferrostaal's compliance with anti-corruption legislation in Germany, which had found that Ferrostaal – part of the German consortium that won the South African submarine contract – had made 'questionable and improper payments' in the course of many of its largest and highest profile projects including the South African submarine deal.

Paul Holden, Feinstein and Van Vuuren called the report an 'outrage'. The commission, they declared, was a unique opportunity to fully investigate the arms deal, to tell the truth to the South African public, and see justice done. 'The result of the Commission's work is exactly the opposite: more prevarication, less truth, no justice.'

Bantu Holomisa, leader of the United Democratic Movement (UDM), said the commission's work had resulted in 'another white-washed report whose objective is nothing less than clearing comrades from Luthuli House'. The Durban High Court was shown evidence alleging arms deal bribes to the then deputy president of the country from the French arms giant Thales. 'This piece of evidence was successfully admitted, used in court and led to the conviction of Mr Schabir Shaik. In the judgment that followed, Mr Zuma was implicated. It is very disturbing that the report is conspicuously quiet on this.'

In an editorial entitled 'Arms deal gets a coat of white-wash', the *Mail & Guardian* wrote that the Seriti report was the whitewash many had predicted. But few had foreseen just how comprehensively it would 'bleach out the slightest taint of government wrongdoing'.

For the government and the governing party, Seriti's 'feeble report' represented the closing of the chapter. They would no doubt be pleased that the commission had found there should be no further official investigations. But an enormous body of evidence had been generated to indicate that politicians, high officials and 'consultants' had cashed in corruptly, and this remained in the public arena.

Journalists and activists would keep digging, said the news-paper, and there was a strong possibility that civil society would challenge Seriti's findings. 'The ANC has welcomed the report. But it may not be the last word.'

Indeed, it would not be. By June 2016, when this book went to press, Crawford-Browne was contemplating a return to the Constitutional Court, and Accountability Now, in conjunction with other civil society organisations, were formulating a sep-arate action to have the arms deal invalidated or cancelled.

The proposed action concentrated on the biggest of the arms deals, that with BAe. In terms of this deal, Hawk and Gripen fighter jets were acquired at a cost of R35 billion at 2015 currency levels, including interest accrued and with provision for fluctuations in the value of currency. The BAe deal is not only the biggest but also the most discussed in the books and documents generated in the wake of the arms deals. Gripen fighter jets are manufactured in Sweden, but in this instance BAe had procured them as well. One of the big advantages of picking on the BAe deal was that all the relevant documents were in English, while many of the internal documents about the other deals were in French, German and Italian. This made it a lot easier to build a case.

In essence, we teased out three main causes of action. The first claim was based on the constitutional requirement that all public procurement must be fair, equitable, transparent, competitive, and cost-effective. The facts suggested that the BAe deal was none of these. The second claim was more technical in nature, and centred on the government's failure to comply with legal requirements for taking the loan from Barclays plc which funded the deal with BAe.

If either of these two claims succeeded, the deal would need to be declared invalid. The aircraft would have to be returned to the British, and the money to the South African taxpayer. The beauty of this was that all of the off-colour aspects of the deals, the bribery and corruption, the unmet off-sets and job opportunities for South African workers were built into the price that would have to be repaid in full. There would be no need to chase after the middle-men and other carpet-baggers; the entire contract price would need to be refunded. The bribes would need to be recovered by the arms dealers themselves –

if they could. In South African law, someone who pays a bribe can't go to court to reclaim it.

The third claim is that the deal was tainted by bribery and criminality which would also provide grounds for its cancellation, not only in terms of the common law but in terms of the procurement agreement itself.

The three claims were set out in greater detail in draft particulars of claim, effectively against the South African government and the Armaments Corporation of South Africa (or Armscor). By late 2016, at the time of going to press, these particulars of claim were being prepared for submission to the North Gauteng High Court. The final particulars of claim as issued in due course will be uploaded to Accountability Now's website (www.accountabilitynow.org.za).

Chapter 6

Polokwane, the Scorpions, and Glenister I

———⊪———

'Be the change you want to see in the world.'
– Mahatma Gandhi

I FIRST met Bob Glenister in February 2008 at the breakfast buffet of the Protea Hotel in Illovo, Johannesburg, which shares a parking area with the Wanderers Club. Given our respective schedules, a breakfast meeting was all we could manage. Bob, a business person, was based in Johannesburg; I was based in Cape Town, and visited Johannesburg infrequently. At that time, I was still director of the CFCR, and our panel of experts was due to meet at the club later that morning. That is why I was in Johannesburg, and briefly available to meet Bob.

Bob's attorney, Kevin Louis of the firm Wertheim Becker, had phoned me and asked me to meet Bob about the ANC's resolution – passed at its national conference at Polokwane a few weeks previously – to dissolve the Directorate of Special Operations (DSO), or Scorpions, the anti-corruption unit based in the National Prosecuting Authority (NPA), and replace it with a unit based in the SAPS.

Bob, like many right-thinking South Africans, was horrified. He was also concerned about the leadership change at

Polokwane, where the 'Zuma tsunami' had ousted the Mbeki team. As a businessman with a considerable investment in South Africa, he feared the worst if the state machinery for combating corruption were to be watered down, and was so appalled by this prospect that he was prepared to do something about it. But what? This was the issue we met to discuss.

In *The Dream Deferred*, the Mbeki biography released in November 2007 – just before Polokwane – Mark Gevisser had written: '. . . I knew, from his confidantes, that Mbeki was deeply distressed by the possibility of being succeeded by Zuma, and that he believed his deputy's play for the presidency to be part of a strategy to avoid prosecution. ... Mbeki allegedly worried that Zuma and his backers had no respect for the rule of law, and would be unaccountable to the constitutional dispensation the ANC had put into place if they came to power . . . For Mbeki and those around him, a Zuma presidency was a scenario far worse than a dream deferred. It would be, in effect, a dream shattered, irrevocably, as South Africa turned into yet another post-colonial kleptocracy . . .'

By the time I met Bob for breakfast, a Zuma presidency was a racing certainty. This was because of the relationship between the national and ANC presidencies, and how this got out of sync at Polokwane. Or, more accurately, how Mbeki sought to disrupt this relationship, and it got back in sync – albeit brutally – at Polokwane.

The South African president is elected by parliament at its first sitting after a general election. While, in theory, any member of parliament could be elected, this effectively means the ANC elects its president. The ANC president, in turn, is elected by the ANC's national conference, which is also held every five years. So is the party's deputy president, who (in terms of the template established by Mandela's succession) is meant to succeed the party president, and eventually ascend to the national presidency.

Mbeki and Zuma were elected as ANC president and deputy president in 1997, and re-elected in 2002. They were also elected as national president and deputy president in 1999, and re-elected in 2004. Due to the two-term limitation in the constitution, Mbeki's national presidency would expire in 2009. However, there was no term limit on the ANC presidency. (At Polokwane, the ANC resolved to introduce this as well.)

In ordinary circumstances, Zuma would or should have peacefully succeeded Mbeki at Polokwane, and ascended to the national presidency two years later. However, following Mbeki's dismissal of Zuma as deputy president in June 2005, following the latter's implication in the Shaik corruption trial, Mbeki decided to contest the ANC presidency for an unusual third term.

Had Mbeki won the leadership contest, he would presumably have determined the party's candidate for the national presidency in two years' time, and remained the power behind the national throne. However, a month before our meeting at the Protea Hotel, , the 'Zuma tsunami' (a term coined by Cosatu general secretary Zwelenzima Vavi, then one of the Zuma conspirators, who later bitterly regretted this decision) had swept Mbeki out of the ANC presidency, and his followers out of key positions in the party and subsequently in government.

Like many business people, Bob was worried about the future under the new regime so feared by Mbeki, and was keenly aware that the constitution was the last line of defence. An unrestrained elite would soon steal South Africa blind, bringing all hopes of a happy and prosperous 'rainbow nation' future crashing down with it. Bob views all politicians with a healthy degree of scepticism, but detests crooked ones especially. When he arrived at breakfast, wearing his trademark black leather jacket, he was accompanied by his attorney, Kevin Louis, and Alf Cockrell, his junior counsel. The leader of his legal team, David Unterhalter SC, was out of the country. The subject for discussion was what to do about the impending dissolution of the Scorpions.

Ironically, the Scorpions were a creature of the ANC. The decision to 'urgently establish a special and adequately staffed and equipped investigative unit to deal with all national priority crime, including police corruption' was announced in June 1999 by none other than Thabo Mbeki, newly minted as national president only a week or so before. The nature of the decision and the perceived urgency surrounding it suggested, and still does, that Mbeki was privy to information which indicated that the country needed the Scorpions sooner rather than later.

Following this policy decision, the DSO was devised and established by Bulelani Ngcuka, national director of public prosecutions, and the minister of justice, Penuell Maduna, who later became one of the panel of experts of the CFCR. Staffed by more than 500 people, the Scorpions began operating in September 1999.

The Scorpions worked in terms of a 'troika principle' under which investigators, prosecutors and forensic experts collaborated on dealing with organised crime and corruption. Global experience has taught that criminal prosecutions are vital; there is no doubt that a culture of impunity takes root rapidly when corruption is not investigated and convictions are not secured. The Scorpions set out to combat corruption in a co-ordinated, and therefore more efficient, way.

The literature on susceptibility to corruption is similarly instructive. It shows that 10 per cent of the global population is corrupt, no matter what; 10 per cent is incorruptible, no matter what; and 80 per cent can go either way, depending on the circumstances. This means that, given effective anti-corruption measures, most of the 80 per cent can be deterred from engaging in corrupt activities. If, however, such measures are lacking, the 80 per cent are more likely to succumb to temptation, mainly because they believe they can get away with it. In an African context in particular, this gives rise to a culture of impunity, and the development of post-colonial kleptocracies. The morphing of popular liberation struggles into the politicians' struggle for untrammelled power is the history of much of post-colonial Africa.

By adopting a supreme constitution, including a Bill of Rights, South Africans set out to do better than many of the countries to our north. Significantly, however, the 'Zuma tsunami' also involved another resolution, taken in the interest of the 'constitutional imperative for a single police service', that the Scorpions be dissolved, and that 'members performing policing functions' should fall under the SAPS. Mirroring Mbeki's concerns, but going the other way, the resolution added that the relevant legislative changes should be 'effected as a matter of urgency'.

Was the decision to disband the Scorpions the proverbial

'canary in the coal mine', a warning that the country was veering away from the rule of law and toward the failed-state status of so many of its neighbours to the north? These were the issues weighing on our minds as the summer sun shone on us in the hotel eatery. Bob had a bold strategy in mind: he wanted to use public interest litigation to nip the deviation from the proper administration of criminal justice he saw in the decision to disband the Scorpions in the bud. The problem with this strategy was that, given the doctrine of the separation of powers entrenched in the constitution, the courts usually defer to other spheres of government; when governance problems arise, they like to be approached as a last resort, and not the first.

The Polokwane resolution in respect of the Scorpions amounted to an instruction to the ANC's parliamentary caucus, and ultimately the national executive, to abolish the Scorpions and replace them with a unit in the SAPS. Parliament was still in recess, and the executive had done nothing yet to start the process of dissolving the Scorpions and creating the Hawks. It was conceivable that the executive would not act on the resolution, or that parliament would baulk at passing the necessary legislation. The problem facing deferential judges sitting in the matter Bob had in mind is that they would not know how the processes of law-making would unfold, and whether the Scorpions would in fact be dissolved, and what would be put in place to replace them. The cabinet would need to decide to act on the resolution, and instruct the government law advisers to draft the necessary legislation. The bill would then need to be tabled in the two houses of parliament, referred to the relevant standing committees, returned to the national assembly and the national council of provinces in amended form, voted on, and sent to the president who, if satisfied with its consistency with the constitution, would sign it into law.

In order to persuade a court to intervene, it was necessary for Bob to plead 'exceptional circumstances' in that, once the legislative process had been completed, it would be too late for the courts to intervene in the normal way, and that an urgent intervention in the form of an interdict and declaratory relief was indicated. Determining what 'exceptional circumstances' actually means is like asking about the length of a piece of string. As for being without a remedy, much the same applies: it depends.

Bob was aware that top Scorpions staff were leaving in droves, unimpressed with the prospect of a future in the SAPS, and willing to sacrifice their state pensions for prospects in the private sector. The state had spent a lot of money on training the Scorpions investigators. Some had attended courses at the Federal Bureau of Investigation (FBI) in the United States, and others at Scotland Yard in the United Kingdom. If the Scorpions were dissolved, its accumulated expertise would be dissipated and its institutional memory destroyed, thus fatally undermining the national project of fighting corruption. Almost certainly, the Hawks would not investigate the top politicians in whom the Scorpions were taking an interest. (This has proven to be the case since. The former national police commissioner Jackie Selebi and the Northern Cape politician John Block are the only 'big fish' convicted of corruption since the Scorpions were disbanded. However, both investigations were initiated by the Scorpions.)

In the Protea Hotel, the coffee grew cold as the discussion

heated up in the crucible of arguments on the issues. The law-yers, as they usually do, looked at the downsides of taking on the state. Bob asked me how I rated his chances of success. I replied that unless he took action, he would never know, but that if he did nothing the Scorpions would almost certainly be disbanded and their accumulated expertise dissipated, thus allowing the worst of the rapidly developing feral elite to save their skins.

'Will your centre back us if we take them on?' asked Bob. I replied that it probably would. I explained the non-confronta-tional and co-operative ethos of the CFCR to Bob, and promised him that I would, at the meeting I was about to attend, propose that we participate as *amicus curiae*.

The issues in the case would impact upon the extent of the constitutionally guaranteed independence of the NPA, the efficiency and effectiveness of corruption-busting, and the enjoyment of guaranteed human rights by all. The separation of powers among the judiciary and other arms of government would play a decisive role, our treaty obligations related to combating corruption would be implicated, and the lot of those who depended on the state's social security net would be affected.

Money lost to corruption does not find its way to the poor; it is spent on fast cars, slow horses and loose living. In the first twenty years of democratic South Africa, some R700 billion has been swallowed up by corruption. This is more than twice the amount needed to eliminate the housing backlog of some 2,1 million housing units, and enough to train the competent teachers so badly needed from early childhood development to matric, equip them to teach in their learners' home languages, and work in properly equipped schools and classrooms.

The issues in the case Bob was contemplating, as we asked for more coffee, were huge. It would also almost certainly cost him a lot of money. He fiddled with the sugar sachets, but showed no other signs of nerves about making a call that would change his life and those of many others. 'OK, let's do it,' he said. 'Where do we start?'

A discussion ensued on what he would need to place before the court. Evidence of the motives behind the resolution, information about the rate of attrition among Scorpions staff, and contextual information about the growth of corruption were all needed. Assembling the necessary affidavits would be a massive task. Cockrell and Louis looked at each other with a mixture of alarm and anticipation. The cabinet would probably move more rapidly to implement the 'urgent' ANC resolution than the papers for the case could be prepared. Therefore, it seemed safe to prepare them on the basis that the cabinet decision would be the point of attack. Section 2 of the constitution makes it clear that any law or conduct inconsistent with the constitution is invalid. Therefore, any cabinet decision to forge ahead with dissolving the Scorpions via a legislative process could be characterised as conduct inconsistent with the constitution. I went off to the panel of experts meeting in the Wanderers clubhouse, leaving the other three to sort out the logistics of the huge task Bob had given his lawyers.

I was pleased to find that the members of the panel were also very concerned about the ANC resolution, and supported the idea that the centre should intervene as an *amicus*, should the opportunity present itself. An *amicus* is permitted to join in proceedings if it has something to add to the arguments already ventilated by the antagonists. It also seemed likely that opposition political parties would want to make capital out of the case, and would also seek to intervene as *amici*.

A few weeks later, Bob found himself in the coffee shop below Kevin Louis's office in Hyde Park, Johannesburg. He was asked to wait there as the final touches were being put on the founding affidavit. By then, the cabinet had indeed decided to initiate the legislation needed to disband the Scorpions, and the case was built around assailing this decision as unconstitutional. Bob was now more aware of the huge and intimidating extent of the challenge. He hesitated and pondered. He felt the need for a sign, so he selected a sugar sachet at random from a bowl on the coffee shop counter, and read the inspirational quote on the back. The quote on his sachet read: 'Be the change you want to see in the world – Mahatma Ghandi.'

This was all Bob needed; he swore to the founding affidavit without further hesitation. He was taking on the full might of the state, in an urgent application to the North Gauteng High Court in Pretoria to stop the dissolution of the Scorpions with immediate effect. He was paying his legal team top dollar to argue the case, in the knowledge that if he did not proceed, the Scorpions would almost certainly be destroyed, with significant consequences for the country's future.

The first step was an urgent application, brought in March in the North Gauteng High Court, for an interdict restraining the government from initiating legislation that would disestablish the DSO. The application was brought by Bob, with the African Christian Democratic Party, Democratic Alliance, Independent Democrats, United Democratic Front, and Inkatha Freedom Party as *amici curiae*.

Predictably, the state's legal representatives argued every technical point available to them. After reserving judgement, Justice Willem van der Merwe delivered his judgement at the end of May. A strong argument, he said, had been made on the applicant's behalf that this was an exceptional case in which the separation of powers should be ignored, and a court should interfere with the right of the executive to initiate legislation. A High Court should only interfere in this way in exceptional circumstances, and the facts in this case did not make it an exceptional one.

Besides this, the matter involved crucial political matters. Given these two factors, the High Court had no jurisdiction to decide the application. However, he said, it 'could fall within the jurisdiction of the Constitutional Court'. In line with this finding, the application was struck off the roll.

Bob was spared the costs of paying for opposing counsel. All the parties agreed that, because the matter was constitutionally significant, no order as to costs should be made. This effectively meant that Bob would pay his own legal team, and the state respondents would pay theirs. Bob's team immediately drafted an application for leave to appeal to the Constitutional Court, alternatively seeking direct access.

Following this ruling, parliament continued to process the bills drafted to give effect to the Polokwane resolution, and the subsequent cabinet decision to implement the resolution. This process involved the appointment of a joint ad hoc committee drawn from the police and justice portfolio committees in the National Assembly. This procedure was necessary as amending the law in respect of the NPA involved the justice portfolio committee, while establishing a new unit in the SAPS – to be called the Directorate for Priority Crime Investigation (DPCI), or Hawks – involved the portfolio committee on police.

Bob organised a petition which was eventually signed by more than 100 000 people. He went to parliament, and made representations to the joint committee. So did the CFCR, the HSF, the Institute for Democracy in South Africa (Idasa), and even a Concerned Members Group from within the NPA. All these interventions were to no avail; ANC MPs were only interested in how best to implement the Polokwane resolution, and not in whether it was constitutional, rational or desirable.

Maggie Sotyu, co-chair of the joint parliamentary committee, in particular, was not interested in hearing submissions regarding the advisability of the scheme to shut down the Scorpions, and only wanted to hear how this could best be done. The constitutionality of depriving the country of its independent and effective anti-corruption machinery of state and the impact of this on its place in the world as well as its international obligations were of no concern to her. An instruction from the party bosses in Luthuli House was on the table, and it was her job to put it into effect.

This kind of conduct, widely referred to as the 'rubberstamping' of executive decisions, has the effect of weakening parliament as an oversight and accountability body to which the cabinet and the public administration are answerable, and this has certainly happened in South Africa. Our weak parliament is a direct result of the proportional representation system utilised for national and provincial elections, in terms of which citizens do not vote for candidates in their own constituencies but for a political party, which chooses its own candidates. This does not happen at the local government level, where people vote for ward councillors as well as parties.

This national and provincial voting system has been in place since 1994. Initially provided for in the interim constitution, it was meant to be a stop-gap measure that which would allow the 1994 elections to proceed in the simplest possible way. The final constitution carried over this system, with minor modifications, to the 1999 elections. In 2002, the government appointed a 13-member electoral task team, chaired by Frederik Van Zyl Slabbert, former leader of the opposition in the apartheid era and co-founder of Idasa, to draft legislation for the 2004 and subsequent elections. The majority of the commissioners proposed a mixed proportional representation and constituency system, similar to that in Germany. However, the government accepted the view of a minority, said to have 'toed the ANC line', that proportional representation should continue. Commenting on the outcome, Slabbert declared it was 'obvious, from the outset, that the government did not really have a serious appetite for changing the system'.

This is hardly surprising, as the current system reduces the accountability of members of parliament to voters in specific constituencies, and makes it easier to force MPs to toe the party line. Besides being nominated by their parties, and the likelihood of their getting into parliament depending on their positions on the party lists, MPs also lose their seats when they cease to be a member of the party on whose list they were elected, unless the floor-crossing schedule to the constitution is invoked. The prospect of losing their parliamentary seats, salaries and fringe benefits works wonderfully to concentrate the minds of parliamentarians, notably including their finding all sorts of reasons for doing exactly what their party bosses tell them to do.

And so it was with the draft legislation to dissolve the Scorpions, and transferring of its functions to the SAPS. The public participation process in parliament was farcical, and the outcome a foregone conclusion. Outside parliament, the secretary-general of the ANC, Gwede Mantashe, openly acknowledged that the motivation for dissolving the Scorpions was that ANC members under investigation by the Scorpions needed to be protected against this intrusion.

This perspective was illuminated by the parliamentary 'Travelgate' scandal, which broke in early 2005. Initially investigated to little effect by the police, but then handed over to the Scorpions, it turned into a major embarrassment for the ANC when scores of its members were compelled to plead guilty to defrauding parliament by abusing their parliamentary travel privileges, to the tune of R18 million. MPs entered into plea bargains that saved them their jobs, on condition that they would pay back the money.

The Constitutional Court heard Bob's application on 20 August 2008. In advance of the hearing, it issued a direction that it wanted to hear argument on only one point, which it framed in a way that did not bode well for Bob's initiative: 'Whether, in the light of the doctrine of the separation of powers, it is appropriate for this court, in all the circumstances, to make any order setting aside the decision of the National Executive that is challenged in this case. The sole question for decision is therefore whether it is appropriate for this court to intervene at this stage of the legislative process.'

The Centre for Constitutional Rights nevertheless decided to participate as an *amicus curiae*, and launched an application to do so with the kind assistance of the pro bono department of the legal firm Bowman Gilfillan. As it seemed likely that the case would be lost but the legislation to follow could still be impugned, we decided to lay the groundwork for the litigation to come by attacking the structural and operational flaws in the new and pending legislation. The UDM also briefed counsel, Michael Osborne of the Cape Bar, to argue the matter as an *amicus*.

Accordingly, there was a host of counsel at court on the morning of 20 August 2008. Chief Justice Pius Langa met us in the ante-room beside the court in his usual friendly and understated way. When I asked after his health, he quietly replied, 'I am well, in spite of the content of the letters you write me' – a wry reference to correspondence about disciplinary proceedings against the Western Cape judge president, John Hlophe. The latter had in May 2008 been accused by all of the judges of the Constitutional Court of interfering with their deliberations on a judgment affecting the rights of Jacob Zuma. The batting order and time allocations were quickly sorted out: Bob's team would go first, followed by the two *amici*. The state would respond after lunch, and Bob's team would get a chance to reply.

It was clear from the outset that the court felt there were

no exceptional circumstances that which would justify intervening in the legislative process at this early stage. David Unterhalter is a skilled and persuasive advocate, but nothing he pulled out of the hat seemed to have an impact.

The Centre for Constitutional Rights was next up. I rose with trepidation. Again, nothing I said seemed to make the slightest difference. The justices were not interested in deviating from their default position of deference to the executive and legislative arms of government. My submission that the court should not sit on its hands and do nothing while an institution as valuable as the Scorpions was being destroyed by a resolution passed for the basest of reasons only seemed to irritate the judges further.

Michael Osborne rose next, with similar results. While he was arguing, Alf Cockrell lent over to me and said, *sotto voce*, that the fate of the Scorpions was sealed. It therefore came as a surprise when, after lunch, Justices Zac Yacoob and Kate O'Regan sharply criticised the way in which counsel for the state had argued its case. Justice Yacoob was particularly severe in respect of a mendaciously worded affidavit by the then director general of the Department of Justice, Menzi Simelane. Simelane later became the first national director of public prosecutions in the Zuma administration, only to be unceremoniously deposed by the courts.

Justice Yacoob felt the deponent was trifling with the court, and voiced his displeasure in no uncertain terms. Eventually, counsel wisely abandoned the contents of Simelane's affidavit, and argued the case on points of law. The separation of powers and the deference the courts owe to the other two main branches of government, the executive and the legislature, formed the basis of the argument presented.

With a good deal of prescience, Justice O'Regan taxed counsel with questions about the effect of the scheme to disband the Scorpions on South Africa's international obligations under the United Nations Convention against Corruption to maintain an effective and independent anti-corruption entity. They assured her that this aspect would be taken into account in drafting the new laws. Nothing that David Unterhalter argued in reply seemed to make an impact. Cases are seldom won on the strength of argument in reply, and it seemed as if Bob's case would not be an exception.

We did not have long to wait for a judgment. The court found – unanimously – that the case was premature. If Bob did not like the end product of the legislative process which was still under way, he was free to return to court after the new laws had been enacted. The decision was written by Chief Justice Langa himself. Acknowledging the wide public interest in the matter, he wrote it in a way that would make the judgment accessible to lay readers as well as lawyers.

After reviewing the factual background, Chief Justice Langa stated that the court was dealing with the constitutionally mandated power of the executive to initiate legislation, and the power of the legislature to enact it. Reasons for justifying intervention by the Constitutional Court in this instance should at least demonstrate material and irreversible harm that could not be remedied once the legislation had been enacted.

The applicant had argued that judicial intervention was appropriate because of the negative effect the draft legislation

on the daily operations of the DSO. In particular, the applicant's counsel had pointed to information that many DSO
employees had resigned, and argued that this was occurring
because of the plan to dis-establish the DSO. The move would
have a material and irreversible effect on the Scorpions, undermine the State's capacity to render basic security, and harm the
constitutional order. There would be no remedy in the future,
because by then it would be too late.

First, Chief Justice Langa noted, this argument was premised
on the assumption that the legislation would be enacted without material change. However, parliament might choose to
amend the legislation, or not enact it at all. Second, it was not
clear that members of the DSO were leaving because of the
decision to dis-establish the Scorpions. Even if they were, this
would not necessarily constitute irreversible harm sufficient
to warrant intervention. Institutions often experienced times
of change and uncertainty as well as high levels of staff turn-
over, which in this instance were not extreme enough to warrant intervention.

The applicant had also argued that the president and cabinet were seeking to disestablish the DSO because a number of
ANC members had received its unwelcome attentions. Again
if this argument had any foundation, appropriate relief could
be sought in due course.

The UDM had argued that the executive was following the
dictates of the governing party rather than its responsibilities
in terms of the constitution. In his view, Chief Justice Langa
noted, there was nothing wrong with the cabinet seeking to give
effect to the policy of the governing party. In so doing, however,

the cabinet had to observe its constitutional obligations. If the eventual legislation breached the constitution, it could be declared invalid.

The UDM had also argued that, having regard to what it refers to as "the relative marginalisation of the legislature" and the dangers of one-party domination, the court should act because no one else would. Chief Justice Langa could not agree. 'The role of this court, he wrote, 'is established in the constitution. It may not assume powers that are not conferred upon it. Moreover, the considerations raised by the UDM do not establish that irreversible and material harm will eventuate should the court not intervene at this stage.'

Lastly, the CFCR had argued that the draft legislation posed a significant threat to the independence of the NPA, and would harm the structure of the constitution. This argument assumed that the draft legislation would remain unchanged during its passage through parliament. The court could not make this assumption, and had to proceed on the basis that parliament would observe its constitutional duties. If the draft legislation did threaten structural harm to the constitution or the NPA, parliament would have a duty to prevent such harm, and it would be inappropriate for the court to intervene in the process of law-making on the assumption that parliament would not observe its constitutional obligations. Again, should the legislation turn out to be unconstitutional, appropriate relief could be obtained thereafter.

Given this, the applicant had not established that it was appropriate for the court to intervene in the affairs of parliament in this case, and had not shown that material and irreversible harm would result if the court did not intervene. In the circumstances, both the application for leave to appeal and the application for direct access to the Constitution Court were refused.

While the judgment had run against us, it opened the door for a determined litigant to take the matter further once the legislation had found its way on to the statute book. Although it was a victory for the government, it was a victory on the narrowest possible basis, with the court declining the make any unnecessary findings in refusing the relief claimed by Bob. All of the arguments concerning the validity, legality and constitutionality of the scheme to disband the Scorpions and replace them with the Hawks were still very much alive. While the government had won the first battle, the war would continue.

Chapter 7

Glenister II, and a meeting under the Flying Arch

———•·•———

'There is always strength in numbers. The more indi-viduals or organisations that you can rally to your cause, the better.'

– Mark Shields

AFTER THE Constitutional Court's adverse judgment in what is widely referred to as 'Glenister I' in October 2008, the government proceeded more cautiously with the two bills needed to shut down the Scorpions and redeploy its investigators in a new unit in the SAPS.

Although the Polokwane resolution stated that the Scorpions should be urgently dissolved, the government still had to adhere to the law. In line with the Freedom Charter, the spiritual foundation of South Africa's inclusive democracy adopted at Kliptown in 1955, a degree of participatory democracy – embodied in its famous phrase 'the people shall govern' – is entrenched in the constitution, among other things by providing members of the public with an opportunity to participate in the legislative process. In practice, this means that, when new laws are made, interested parties may make written and oral submissions to the relevant parliamentary portfolio committees. In order to facilitate this, details of the legislation as well as the public hearings are advertised in the media.

While, in Glenister I, the Constitutional Court had found that the specific circumstances did not warrant its intervention in the workings of parliament and the legislative process, it did acknowledge in principle that it could intervene. Apparently, those in authority interpreted this as a warning that the public participation aspect of making these new laws would need to be in apple-pie order.

This had the effect of holding up the legislative process into 2009, by which time the ANC had recalled President Thabo Mbeki, and Kgalema Motlanthe was acting as 'caretaker' president pending the general elections in 2009. Despite strong opposition from the minority parties, parliament eventually passed the two bills, and Motlanthe signed them into law in February 2009 (shortly after advising former president F W de Klerk and Archbishop Desmond Tutu that if they had any evidence of corruption or other malfeasance in the arms deals, they should report it to the police).

These new laws did not sit well with Bob Glenister, but he was reluctant to spend more money on additional litigation. It is rare for a litigant who has lost a major case to go back to court at a later stage. Bob had an arguable case in Glenister I, and his intentions were pure, but the courts were not prepared to find that the circumstances were exceptional enough to justify its intervention in the legislative process before the laws had reached the statute book. However, both Justice Willem van der Merwe and Chief Justice Pius Langa had effectively suggested that the new laws could be scrutinised afresh once they had been placed on the statute book, to see whether they passed constitutional muster.

On the day the new laws were gazetted, Bob's attorney, Kevin Louis, spoke to me on the phone. During the conversation, I said: 'In my view, Bob has paid for his ticket, and should be entitled to see the show. We wouldn't expect him to pay us, but the institute could assist him by finding lawyers who would act for him on contingency. Are you up for it?'

Kevin was available to act as the attorney of record in Johannesburg, and Bob was willing to enter into a contingency arrangement with our legal team. I asked Peter Hazell SC, a retired member of the Cape Bar, to assist, and he readily agreed. Callie Albertyn of De Klerk and Van Gend, who had acted for the UDM in Glenister I, was prepared to come on board as the Cape Town attorney of record, also acting on a contingency basis.

Bob assembled a full legal team with the minimum of fuss. We fondly imagined that we would be supported by others once the matter got going with numerous *amicus* interventions, as had been the case in the first round of Bob's legal adventures aimed at saving the Scorpions. In the event, this did not come to pass – once bitten, twice shy seemed to be the order of the day. Other non-government organisations with mandates similar to those of Accountability Now were openly sceptical about Bob's chances of success. The opposition political parties were conspicuously absent. In fact, the DA's shadow minister of justice, Dene Smuts, scornfully described Accountability Now as a 'one man and a fax machine', using this as part of a justification for staying out of the fray. We never consisted of one person only, and we have certainly never owned a fax machine, a relic of an era long past by the time Accountability Now was formed. Smuts was taken to task by Chris Barron in the *Sunday Times*, and admitted later that the successes of Accountability Now had forced her to eat her words at many a dinner party. Sadly, she died suddenly in April 2016.

Peter Hazell and I sat down and surveyed the pile of paper that had been generated in the course of Glenister I. It was impressively large, created by a talented and skilled team of lawyers in Johannesburg. It was certainly not for lack of trying that the case, in its first round, had not succeeded. The assembled facts alone would be a huge help in preparing the new challenge.

Bob had a choice: both the North Gauteng High Court in Pretoria and the Western Cape High Court in Cape Town have jurisdiction in reviews of this kind, as the legislature is based in Cape Town and the executive in Pretoria. Given his bad luck when he first took the case to Pretoria, Bob decided to sue in the Western Cape High Court. A direct approach to the Constitutional Court was ruled out; nothing could be worse than going from Braamfontein to Cape Town and back to Braamfontein, which is what could happen if a direct approach to the Constitutional Court was attempted and rejected.

Preparing the founding papers was relatively simple; all we had to do was rehash much of what had been argued before, and add some new information. The fresh information largely had to do with the passage of the two bills through parliament, and their final content when they were signed into law. Any law that is inconsistent with the constitution is invalid. Again, we would ask the court to declare the laws dissolving the Scorpions and establishing the Hawks as invalid.

Peter Hazell and I spent long hours reworking the founding affidavit, and examining the constitutionality of the two laws from every conceivable angle. In public interest litigation of this kind, it is best to leave no stone unturned. The court may like a point you think is weak, and reject a point you regard as a winning one. The law is as unpredictable as the weather in Port Elizabeth, and just as windy.

We decided that the human resource management aspect of the case might benefit from an expert opinion. In our view, a perfectly good system, the Scorpions, located in the NPA, was being replaced by a deeply flawed one, the Hawks, located in the SAPS. In the process of doing so, members of the Scorpions would receive such a raw deal that the new law could be regarded as an unfair labour practice. Fair labour practices are constitutionally guaranteed. The state is obliged to respect, protect, promote and fulfil fair labour practices along with all the other human rights guaranteed in the Bill of Rights.

Fortunately, Daan Groeneveldt, an experienced practitioner in the human resources management field, was a co-founder of Accountability Now. He was able to produce a thoughtful analysis of the reporting lines of the Scorpions compared with those of the Hawks, in order to demonstrate the relative independence of the former and the relative lack of independence of the latter. It was all a matter of the contrasting sapiential authority (a fancy term for 'clout') of the two units. According to Daan, the lack of gravity apparent in the structure of the Hawks would undermine its independence, and accordingly its functional effectiveness. In the process, the ethos of the Scorpions that had inspired its members and driven them to a high and growing success rate in combating corruption in high and low places would be destroyed.

After much effort, the papers were finalised and served on the usual government respondents. Not unexpectedly, the matter was opposed. Counsel on both sides swiftly approached the deputy judge president of the Western Cape High Court with a view to obtaining an early date for a hearing. The court agreed, and, given the seriousness and urgency of the case, also agreed that it should be heard by a full bench of three judges. A timetable was set up for exchanging further affidavits and for filing heads of argument. Willie Duminy SC, briefed by the State Attorney, ably led the team for the state, and was very co-operative prior to the hearing. The hearing itself was allocated to Judges Siraj Desai, Burton Fourie and Dumisani Zondi.

It did not start well. As the three judges filed into court, Duminy slid a pile of paper across the desk towards me, muttering that he had forgotten to give it to me earlier. It was an application to strike out much of the material we had placed before the court. This device is resorted to when allegedly irrelevant or inadmissible material has been placed on record. I was taken aback by the tardiness of the state team, but told the court that, in view of the urgency of the matter, and the degree of public interest, we would respond to the striking-out application without seeking a postponement. The court accepted this, and heard argument from both sides on the merits of the case and on the striking-out application – in which the admissibility and relevance of Bob's evidence was under attack – over the next few days. Besides attacking the rationality of replacing the hugely effective Scorpions with an unknown entity that would be housed in a dysfunctional police service, we assailed the legislative scheme in every conceivable way.

The judgment took nine months to prepare, but was short and to the point. The legislative scheme was deemed to be rational, and the other points raised were beyond the jurisdiction of the High Court. Effectively, the three Cape judges replicated Justice Van Der Merwe's finding in the North Gauteng High Court two years previously. The judgment was handed down by Judge Desai, with the concurrence of his colleagues. It summarised our arguments as follows:

- Lack of rationality;
- Absence of accountability;
- Failure of sound human resource management;
- Breach of international obligations;
- Failure to ensure proper public participation in the law-making process;
- Infringement of the obligation not to undermine the human rights values enshrined in the Bill of Rights; and
- Failure to allow the NPA to properly exercise its functions.

All of these arguments, except for rationality, were neatly side-stepped by the jurisdiction issue, which Duminy had argued and the court had accepted. The Court did not deal with the striking-out application at all. However, given the public interest nature of the litigation, it also made no order for costs, and expressly rejected a government contention that Bob was being vexatious by pursuing the case after having lost in the Constitutional Court.

It was, in fact, time to take the case back to the Constitutional Court. We prepared the necessary papers, and encountered the usual opposition. Strangely, the striking-out application did not resurface; it was unclear whether this was by design or due to an oversight. We weren't going to ask; the case was difficult enough without a side-show about possibly striking out much of the material that had so painstakingly been placed on record on Bob's behalf.

While the case was pending, I had a chance encounter with Raenette Taljaard, a recent executive director of the Helen Suzman Foundation (HSF), at the Idasa offices in Cape Town. She was a guest speaker at a function I attended, and afterwards we chatted together amiably under a remarkable art installation in Idasa's Dakar Room. Entitled 'The Flying Arch', it depicts Archbishop Emeritus Desmond Tutu swinging from a chandelier in joy at the freedom guaranteed by South Africa's new constitutional order. (Idasa had commissioned the sculpture from the artist Ed Young after an open competition. Following the organisation's unfortunate closure in 2013, it was first sold to a private buyer, and resold on auction in 2015.)

Raenette, previously the youngest member in the first parliament in the new South Africa, had worked hard to help oppose the two bills. On behalf of the HSF, she had engaged the legal firm Webber Wentzel to help draft submissions to the parliamentary joint committee aimed at alerting it to the unconstitutionality and folly of the ANC's course of action. Webber Wentzel allocated the brief to a senior partner and former politician, Peter Leon, brother of the then leader of the opposition, Tony Leon. Peter's argument for retaining the Scorpions fell on deaf ears, as did all other submissions opposing the legislation. The ANC cadres in parliament were also not moved by the petition Bob had organised, and the antipathy in the media had no discernible effect on the resolute pursuit of their goal. They stuck to the task of putting the Polokwane resolution into practice, and commanded a sufficient majority in parliament to do so.

Raenette herself had put a lot of effort into the HSF submission to parliament. She had previously served on SCOPA, and still bore the scars of the arms deal cover-up which she had witnessed and sought to prevent at first hand. Her concern about the role of burgeoning corruption in undermining South Africa's constitutional democracy prompted her to take an active interest in the debate about the Scorpions.

As we chatted under the benevolent gaze of the swinging Arch, she asked how the Glenister case was progressing. I bewailed our inability to persuade any local organisations to join the fray as *amici*. 'Have you asked my successor at the HSF, Francis Antonie?' she asked. I replied that I hadn't, despite her contribution to the debate in parliament.

'Well,' she retorted, 'the HSF spent a great deal of money on that debate, and it ought to follow through with at least an *amicus* intervention now that the case has reached the Constitutional Court for the second time.'

I took her comment home with me, and decided to write an email to Antonie, copied to Peter Leon. The worst that could happen would be a 'Sorry, no', or no reply at all. I worded the email very carefully, drawing attention to the HSF's investment in public participation in the parliamentary proceedings, and encouraging them to follow through on their commitment to the cause. Rather cheekily, I even suggested that if Webber Wentzel would not help on a pro bono basis, I could find lawyers who would be honoured to do so. Lastly, I suggested that the case could best be beefed up in the areas of human rights infringements and international obligations.

The email had the desired effect. The HSF assembled a highly talented legal team, with Webber Wentzel as instructing attorneys, marshalled interns to thoroughly investigate the international ramifications of the case, and generally put its full weight and good reputation behind it.

This type of intervention is invaluable to a lone warrior such as Bob. The suggestion, either real or imaginary, express or implied, that a quixotic litigant is tilting at windmills always stalks public interest litigants who take matters to court in their own name. The fervour of the crusader or jihadist tends to alienate the sound and sober pillars of the community. The default position of many people who have grown up under an authoritarian regime is simply to acquiesce in what those in authority do and say.

There is not much appetite in the new order for doing the right thing, when you've been told to do the wrong thing. Intelligent disobedience is in short supply. Bob is an exception, and was fortunate to be assisted by the HSF, as a result of a chance conversation at a chance meeting under the Flying Arch in the Dakar room at Idasa. At least Idasa, which no longer exists, can take credit for providing the venue and arranging the occasion on which the chance conversation between Raenette and me took place.

The HSF team took up my suggestion, and concentrated their attention on human rights infringements and international law obligations as the strongest weapons in Bob's arsenal. On the international obligations aspect, they assembled all the anti-corruption treaties and conventions to which South Africa is a party, and pointed to provisions that would be breached by replacing the Scorpions with the Hawks. On the human rights infringement aspect, they drew attention to each provision of the Bill of Rights that would or could be implicated in or threatened by the substitution.

The Chief Justice of the Constitutional Court – now Chief Justice Sandile Ncgobo – set down the case for hearing on 2 September 2010. By then, the HSF team had been allowed to participate as friends of the court, and had filed comprehensive arguments on the two points we had asked them to address. Only nine judges were available. As we waited for them to file in at the start of the hearing, there was much speculation as to which judges would incline in favour of which party. This normally becomes apparent from the drift of the questions members of the bench direct at counsel in the course of the hearing.

It was my duty – and honour – to start the argument. I took the court through the bones of the case, tersely setting out the points that had already been argued in the Western Cape High Court, knowing full well that the judges would ask a lot of questions, and that I would not have much time to deal with them. It soon became apparent that some of the judges were interested in the human rights ramifications, while others asked pointed questions about the impact on South Africa's international obligations. David Unterhalter SC, who had represented Bob in Glenister I back in 2008, was next up on behalf of the HSF. He provided the answers to the questions about the two prominent issues, and his team had placed a great deal of material about the international law aspects of the case before the court.

Willie Duminy SC, who had the task of replying to our arguments, realised from the tenor of the questions streaming into the crucible of argument that the government's case was in trouble. He found some sympathy from the bench, particularly from Acting Justice Fritz Brand, a former colleague at the Cape Bar and on secondment from the Supreme Court of Appeal. Questions about the adequacy of the independence of the Hawks were discussed, and the international law aspects of the case became obfuscated. In a last throw of the dice, Duminy decided to try to reintroduce the application to strike out material in Bob's founding affidavit. The Chief Justice would have none of this; he firmly declined to accept the wad of paper offered by Duminy, and nothing further was heard on the topic.

By the time the court adjourned at the end of argument, Unterhalter was upbeat. He thought enough of the judges were with us to secure a majority in favour of the proposition that the two laws should be declared invalid. I wasn't sure. Some judges are inscrutable, whether by nature or by design, and the scales were too evenly balanced to be certain of a majority either way. My nervousness was compounded a few weeks later when the court called for additional written argument on the international law aspects of the case. We duly complied, and quickly filed answers to the points raised. The wait for judgment began. We warned Bob, who had attended the hearing, that the result could go either way, but that the chances of his being ordered to pay costs were slim.

Bob did not believe us. So, when the date of judgment – 17 March 2011 (perhaps a nod to my Irish ancestry, it is St Patrick's Day) – was announced, he put on his best suit, tucked his cheque book into the breast pocket, and went to court fully expecting to be asked to pay the government's costs in the matter on the grounds that he had wasted so much of its time.

To Bob's great surprise, the judges divided five to four in his favour on the question of whether the Hawks were fully equipped to fulfil the task previously carried out by the Scorpions. All the judges were agreed that it was legally in order to dispense with the services of the Scorpions; four thought the Hawks were an adequate replacement, but five did not. A partial win was better than no win at all. When the court order was being read out, and its import dawned on him, a look of incredulity (later publicly remarked on by Justice Edwin Cameron) spread over Bob's face. His cheque book remained firmly in his pocket.

Parliament was given 18 months to take remedial steps to create an effective and adequately independent substitute for the Scorpions. The business end of the order read: 'It is declared that Chapter 6A of the South African Police Service Act 68 of 1995 is inconsistent with Constitution, and invalid to the extent that it fails to secure an adequate degree of independence for the Directorate for Priority Crime Investigation. The declaration of constitutional invalidity is suspended for 18 months in order to give Parliament the opportunity to remedy the defect.'

A media release accompanying the judgment, handed down on 17 March 2011, said the key question in this case was whether the national legislation that created the Directorate for Priority Crime Investigation (DPCI), known as the Hawks, and disbanded the Directorate of Special Operations (DSO), known as the Scorpions, was constitutionally valid. The majority of the Court found that Chapter 6A of the South African Police Services Act 68 of 1995, as amended, was inconsistent with the Constitution, and invalid to the extent that it failed to secure an adequate degree of independence for the DPCI.

The Court had made two key findings. First, it held that the Constitution imposed an obligation on the state to establish and maintain an independent body to combat corruption and organised crime. While the Constitution did not in express terms command that a corruption-fighting unit should be established, its scheme taken as a whole imposed a pressing duty on the state to set up a concrete, effective and independent mechanism to prevent and root out corruption. This obligation was sourced in the Constitution and the international law agreements which were binding on the state.

'The Court points out,' the release said, 'that corruption undermines the rights in the Bill of Rights, and imperils our democracy.' Section 7(2) of the Constitution imposed a duty on the state to respect, protect, promote and fulfil the rights in the Bill of Rights. When read with section 8(1), which provides that the rights in the Bill of Rights bind all branches of government; section 39(1)(b), which provides that Courts must consider international law when interpreting the Bill of Rights; and section 231, which provides that an international agreement that parliament approves binds the Republic, this provision placed an obligation on the state to create an independent corruption-fighting unit.

Parliament had approved a number of international agreements on combating corruption, which were binding on the Republic. These required that states create independent anti-corruption entities. Section 7(2) of the Constitution implied that the steps the state should take to protect and fulfil constitutional rights must be reasonable. To create an anti-corruption unit that was not adequately independent, thereby ignoring binding international law, was not a reasonable constitutional measure.

Second, the Court found that the Hawks did not meet the constitutional requirement of adequate independence. Consequently, the impugned legislation did not pass constitutional muster. The main reason for this conclusion was that the DPCI was insufficiently insulated from political influence in its structure and functioning. This was because its activities would be co-ordinated by Cabinet, as the statute provided that a Ministerial Committee could determine policy guidelines in respect of the functioning of the DPCI, as well as for the selection of national priority offences. This form of oversight made the unit vulnerable to political interference.

Further, the Court held that measures, aimed at protecting the DPCI against political influence and interference, were inadequate. In addition, the conditions of service of the unit's members and in particular those applying to its head made it insufficiently independent. Members had inadequate employment security to carry out their duties vigorously, the appointment of members was not sufficiently shielded from political influence, and remuneration levels were flexible and not secured. These aspects made the unit vulnerable to an undue measure of political influence.

'Hence, the Court upholds the appeal, declares the offending legislative provisions establishing the DPCI constitutionally invalid to the extent that they do not secure adequate independence, and suspends the declaration of constitutional invalidity for a period of eighteen months to give Parliament the opportunity to remedy the defect.'

The minority judgment by Ngcobo CJ, in which Brand AJ, Mogoeng J and Yacoob J concurred, held that section 7(2) of the Constitution, while giving rise to a positive obligation on the state to fight corruption and organised crime, did not specifically impose an obligation on the state to establish an independent corruption-fighting unit. It further held that, insofar as such a constitutional obligation was found, the structural and operational autonomy of the Hawks was secured through institutional and legal mechanisms that were adequately designed to prevent undue interference and safeguard the independence of the DPCI. The minority judgment therefore concluded that the appeal should be dismissed.

Both the majority and the minority judgments concluded that the legislation that created the Hawks could not be invalidated on the grounds that it was irrational, or that parliament had failed to facilitate public involvement in the legislative process. Both judgments further concluded that the constitution did not oblige parliament to locate a specialised corruption-fighting unit within the NPA, and nowhere else.

Another battle against corruption had been fought, and this time partially won, but the war would continue. Bob's cheque book, snugly in his pocket on the day of judgment, would be used in further efforts to secure effective and independent state machinery to combat corruption, and prevent its further spread.

Chapter 8

Stirring the pot after Glenister II

———•———

'A conception of democracy which is committed to a notion of freedom and dignity, self-rule and self-respect must entail a commitment to a form of political practice that guarantees to each person the basic social conditions required for the fulfilment of these commitments.'

– Judge Dennis Davis

LOTS OF noses were put out of joint by the finding of a majority of Constitutional Court judges in what has become known as Glenister II. Besides the government and the ANC, whose noses were properly bloodied, they included the proboscis of those who had confidently predicted that the case could not be won and had therefore declined to have anything to do with it, either as a friend of the court or as co-applicant. Over at Luthuli House, the ANC's headquarters in Johannesburg, secretary-general Gwede Mantashe muttered darkly about 'counter-revolutionary judges', as if any judges sworn to uphold the constitutions of their countries could normally be described as 'revolutionaries'.

Academic commentators pored over the judgment, and marvelled at the scope of its finding that the democratically elected parliament would have to return to the drawing board to create an independent institution of state capable of preventing and combating corruption. The judges had been careful to avoid telling parliament what to do. Instead, they described the internationally accepted attributes of a successful anti-corruption entity: a specialised body of well-trained personnel who would enjoy security of tenure, access to adequate and guaranteed resources and funding, and the room to operate independently, free of executive interference or influence.

These precepts were the criteria against which a constitutionally sound entity would be measured in the future. Clearly, the Hawks did not meet those criteria. The security of its members was questionable. Their vulnerability to executive interference and influence was built into the founding legislation. They were also not specialists in combating corruption. Instead, their mandate was extended to covering 'priority crimes' which – in terms of the legislation – would be defined and selected by the executive, and not the Hawks themselves. Small wonder, then, that the Constitutional Court judges gave parliament a period of eighteen months to think about and implement its ruling.

The victorious parties, Bob Glenister and the HSF, both decided to follow through on the unexpected victory. This seemed to be the most responsible way of utilising the surprise win they had achieved through perseverance and hard work. The HSF organised a workshop to discuss the way forward, which was attended by academics, government officials and representatives of relevant NGOs. Puzzlingly, neither Bob nor his legal team was invited. Accountability Now was also not on the guest list. The workshop was held in private, and the outcome, if any, was not made public.

The HSF did, at a later stage, confer with the Glenister team about the line to take during the renewed public participation process in parliament. After a few conference calls, facilitated by the attorneys acting for the HSF, they agreed to differ. Bob and his team wanted to go for broke and campaign for a new Chapter Nine institution, an Integrity Commission. In his view, such an entity would slot in neatly between the Public Protector, who is mandated to deal with public maladministration, and the Auditor General, who checks government accounts for irregular and wasteful expenditure. A commission with a mandate to prevent and combat corruption in the public and private sectors would fill the gaps left by the public-sector oriented focus of the Auditor General and Public Protector, neither of whom have a mandate to deal with corruption in the private sector.

Team HSF was not as ambitious as Team Glenister; like the DA, it favoured the reintroduction of a Scorpions-like entity. The difficulty with this proposal was that, like the Scorpions, such an entity would not enjoy the same security as Chapter Nine institutions – so named after their enabling chapter in the constitution – established to help bed down South Africa's constitutional democracy. No person may interfere with the functioning of these institutions, and other organs of state are required to assist and protect them in order to ensure their independence, impartiality, dignity and effectiveness. The institutions themselves are enjoined to act impartially, without fear, favour or prejudice. By contrast, the Scorpions could be disbanded because they were creatures of statute, and could be destroyed by the same parliament that had created them. Amending the constitution to create a new Chapter Nine institution would be much more difficult to reverse than ordinary legislation.

Bob decided that the idea of a new Chapter Nine institution needed to be tested in the national marketplace, and put up the funding for what became known as the Glenister Challenge. Participants in three categories – universities, civil society, and an open category – were invited to submit their ideas for remedial legislation, and a memorandum justifying their choices. Three retired judges, Johann Kriegler of the Constitutional Court, Ian Farlam of the Supreme Court of Appeal, and Wilfred Thring of the Western Cape High Court, agreed to adjudicate the entries. A team of communications consultants, led by Dani Cohen and Sandra Sowray of Prolog Consulting, were engaged to get the message into the public domain, and attract as many participants as possible. Law, public administration, and politics departments at universities were asked to interest their students in the project. People active in the private sector could enter in the 'open' section.

A few entrants who tried the one-liner 'Bring back the death penalty' were promptly eliminated, but the overwhelming majority in all categories made a serious effort to formulate a new law, and explain and justify their choices. The competition kept the options in the public eye, and Accountability Now did what it could to reinforce the promotion of an Integrity Commission. This strategy involved writing opinion pieces for newspapers, appearing on radio and television, and talking to audiences as diverse as clubs, universities, and religious organisations.

In the event, the government gave the task of preparing the remedial legislation to the SAPS, which seemed likely to result in a proposal for a 'super-Hawks' unit in the place of the Hawks. The failure to involve the Department of Justice and Constitutional Development in this process seemed to scupper any hopes of creating a new Chapter Nine institution to embody the STIRS (specialised, trained, independent, resourced and secure) criteria spelled out by the Constitutional Court. A unit within the SAPS would fail to meet several of these criteria, notably independence and security.

When the new draft bill was published, it was met with dismay. It seemed aimed at doing as little as possible to meet the requirements of the judgment. Many analysts and role players felt this was not enough, and so did participants in the renewed public participation process. A single participant, a professor at the University of the Witwatersrand, supported the structural and operational changes contained in the bill. All of the other twenty-odd submissions to the police portfolio committee in the National Assembly criticised the bill, and made constructive suggestions for improving it.

The universities category in the Glenister Challenge was won by a two-person team from the University of Stellenbosch, pipping a Rhodes University team at the post. In the civil society section, the team of Ndifuna Ukwazi (Dare to Know), part of the Social Justice Coalition stable, prevailed over its competitors. The challenge was rounded off with a prize-giving party at the Vineyard Hotel in Cape Town, which was enjoyed by all. More soberly, the entries had no impact whatsoever on the government drafting team. It was taking its instructions from Luthuli House; 'counter-revolutionary judges' were not to be heeded in anything but the most minimal way.

The notion of a majority party in a constitutional democracy being constrained by the separation of powers is greatly misunderstood in the corridors of Luthuli House. There is even less appreciation of the fact that laws and conduct that are inconsistent with the constitution are invalid. Luthuli House firmly believes that a majority party can do what it likes, and the minority (as well as the courts) must bow before its will. President Zuma himself let this slip in an exchange in parliament with the DA's then parliamentary leader, Lindiwe Mazibuko. 'The majority has more rights than the minority,' he declared. 'That is how democracy works.'

But constitutional democracy does not work in that way at all: the constitution means what the Constitutional Court says it means. The courts are independent of political parties, and subject only to the law and the constitution, which they must apply without fear, favour or prejudice. An order or decision issued by a court binds all relevant parties, including organs of state. These notions are clearly and concisely set out in section 165 of the constitution, which says that the state has a duty to 'assist and protect the courts to ensure the independence, impartiality, dignity, accessibility and effectiveness of the courts'.

All of this means that the remedial action ordered by the Constitutional Court had to be consistent with the constitution. The new Hawks legislation failed to measure up to these standards by a country mile. The political will to deal effectively and decisively with corruption remained conspicuously absent. Bob briefed Accountability Now and his new Cape Town-based attorney, Madri du Plessis of the firm Cooper and

Associates, to make representations to the portfolio committee. So did the HSF, and many other leading civil society organisations. Everyone, bar one lonely Wits University professor, warned of the unconstitutionality of the new bill, and Bob asked the committee to send it back to the drawing board. We argued on his behalf that it was impossible to make a silk purse out of a sow's ear, and that the bill was the latter.

The ANC members of the committee had their instructions. Asking them to accept that the bill was fundamentally flawed was like asking them to grow wings and fly. Their very jobs depended upon their supporting it. They did, however, take some civil society criticisms seriously, and introduced about 50 minor amendments. Unfortunately, the amendments tended to compound the confused thinking already embodied in the bill. Warnings that the amended bill still did not pass constitutional muster fell on deaf ears. Clearly, the government was determined to do as little as possible to comply with the STIRS criteria spelled out by the Constitutional Court.

Attempts to involve Chapter Nine institutions – particularly the Human Rights Commission and the Public Protector – in the debate did not succeed. Eventually, the bill passed through both houses of parliament, propelled by the ANC majority. All we could do now, short of litigation, was to ask the president not to sign the bill into law, as it did not comply with the constitution – a power conferred on him by the constitution itself. He could either send the bill back to parliament, or refer it to the Constitutional Court for its imprimatur on the constitutionality of its provisions. Instead, he signed the bill into law, just within the 18-month deadline. The new law made minor changes to the powers of the Hawks, and some cosmetic changes to its structure and functioning.

Working separately, and without consulting one another, Team Glenister and Team HSF considered the new situation, and decided to approach the Constitutional Court directly on the grounds that the new legislation did not meet its criteria, and should therefore be declared unconstitutional. Team HSF adopted a 'lean and mean' approach, based on the text of the new provisions. Team Glenister, while also critical of the text, adopted a broader approach, arguing that, in the circumstances prevailing in the executive, the SAPS and the Hawks themselves, the whole scheme of the new act was unconstitutional. The phrase 'in the circumstances' was drawn from the majority judgment in Glenister II, which stated:

'Now plainly, there are many ways in which the state can fulfil its duty to take positive measures to respect, protect, promote and fulfil the rights in the Bill of Rights. This Court will not be prescriptive as to what measures the state takes, as long as they fall within the range of possible conduct that a reasonable decision-maker in the circumstances may adopt. A range of possible measures is therefore open to the state, all of which will accord with the duty the Constitution imposes, so long as the measures taken are reasonable.'

Team Glenister set out to argue that the new measures were unreasonable, given the state of the executive, populated with feral politicians, and led by a person facing the reinstatement of 783 corruption charges; a dysfunctional police force, which was mismanaged and poorly led by political appointees; and the parlous position of the Hawks, itself a dysfunctional and mismanaged police unit, led by political appointees under the ANC's notorious cadre deployment policy.

In the event, the Constitutional Court took one look at the two applications, and rejected them summarily without giving either party a hearing. It was not prepared to address the issues before a lower court had done so. So Teams HSF and Glenister rejigged their papers for an approach to the Western Cape High Court, asking it to declare the super-Hawk legislation invalid. Team HSF persisted in its narrow and technical approach, while Team Glenister continued to focus on the unsuitability of locating an anti-corruption entity within the police, besides its technical attacks on the structure of the legislation, and how the new Hawks would be required to function. Another major battle in the war against corruption was about to begin.

Chapter 9

The Constitutional Court drafts legislation

———————

*'Ask not what your country can do for you; ask what
you can do for your country.'*
– John F Kennedy

MADRI DU Plessis must rue the day when she approached me
at the end of a lively question and answer session at a meeting of
the Institute of Arbitrators which I had just addressed. Pressing
her business card into my hand, she asked: 'How can I help you?'

The card stated that she was an attorney, practising in Cape
Town. 'Send me your CV,' I replied; 'I'm sure we can find something that will fit your skills set.'

The CV duly arrived. It was immediately clear that Madri
was ideally suited to serve as the attorney of record for Bob
Glenister in the third round of his litigation aimed at preserv-
ing South Africa's anti-corruption machinery. Besides being a
qualified attorney, she had worked for a firm of solicitors in
London specialising in issues around corruption. Madri went
on to play a central role in the lobbying that preceded Glenister III. She prepared draft legislation of the kind Accountability
Now would like to see on the statute book. She helped to
organise the Glenister Challenge, and to prepare a submission

to the police portfolio committee in the National Assembly. The heavy lifting came when we had to litigate in order to give effect to Bob's instructions, after all lobbying efforts and submissions to parliament had failed.

After the false start in the Constitutional Court, the team assembled to plot the way forward. The High Court was the correct theatre of renewed battle, but which one? As Bob lived in Johannesburg, and members of the legal team in Cape Town and the Eastern Cape, we could choose to go to the North Gauteng High Court or the Western Cape High Court. Both Pretoria and Cape Town are seats of government, and both have jurisdiction in matters in which the constitutionality of legislation is impugned. That is what makes these two courts so unpopular among senior ANC staff stationed in Luthuli House.

As the work would be done mainly in Cape Town, we decided to proceed there. Bob did not have fond memories of the first round of his case in the North Gauteng High Court, and was relaxed about the matter proceeding in Cape Town even though he had lost there too in Glenister II, prior to the reversal of that decision in the Constitutional Court.

Unbeknown to Team Glenister, the HSF had also decided to proceed in the Western Cape High Court despite being based in Johannesburg, with a legal team drawn partly from Durban and partly from Johannesburg. Despite differences in approach, both teams were ready to issue process in Cape Town at the end of 2012. Team HSF confined its attack on the new legislation to a narrow and objective examination of the text, while Team Glenister took up the invitation of the Constitutional Court to attend to the circumstances relevant to the new law.

This approach takes the context of a piece of legislation into account in judging its contents, while the 'objective' approach confines itself to legal issues. Both approaches have their place. More specifically, due regard for 'the circumstances', identifies the mischief which the legislation in question is intended to address. The mischief in this case was corruption, and how best to combat it. The extent of corruption in the society for which the law was intended then becomes a relevant consideration. Sledgehammers are not used to kill fleas; nor should one go to a gunfight armed with a knife. In this instance, the extent of corruption in government, the police, the Hawks, and the executive branch of government in particular would be relevant.

When Bob first approached the Constitutional Court in an effort to save the Scorpions, he referred to a meeting between Helen Zille, then leader of the DA, and Gwede Mantashe, ANC secretary-general, in April 2008. Mantashe is arguably the most powerful person in the ANC; some even call him South Africa's unofficial prime minister. During a two-hour meeting in Luthuli House, he made four points that are worth repeating.

Firstly, he reportedly declared, the ANC wanted the Scorpions disbanded because they were a 'political unit made up of apartheid security branch members who treated the ANC like the enemy'. Secondly, its continued investigation of Jacob Zuma was an 'abuse of power'. Thirdly, the ANC would ensure that its Polokwane resolution to disband the Scorpions was implemented. Lastly, the ANC wanted the Scorpions disbanded because they were 'prosecuting ANC leaders'.

By the time that Glenister III was launched, the Scorpions

had indeed been disbanded, and the prosecution of allegedly crooked ANC leaders had stopped. The late Jackie Selebi, former commissioner of police, and John Block, former ANC leader in the Northern Cape and MEC for finance in its provincial government, were the last ANC 'big fish' convicted of corruption. Both were investigated by the Scorpions.

While fraud and corruption in high places undoubtedly continued, prosecutors and investigators had clearly concluded that pursuing these with the same zeal would be tantamount to putting their necks on the chopping block. Turkeys do not look forward to Christmas. The figures tell the story. In 2008/9, the Hawks' first full year of operation, the number of new investigations fell by 85 per cent over the previous year, and the value of contraband seized by 99 per cent. The raw numbers also make for sobering reading: while, in 2007/8, the Scorpions had seized goods valued at more than R4 billion, in 2008/9 the Hawks seized goods valued at R35 million. These statistics are startling as well as dismaying.

Given the obvious discomfort of some ANC leaders with the attentions of an anti-corruption agency, as indicated by Mantashe, it was reasonable to infer that the executive preferred the level of work done by the Hawks to that of the Scorpions. The figures cited above appeared in the annual reports of the NPA. They did not spark an outrage, fuel a furious debate in parliament, or provoke much public comment. Neither did a reply to a parliamentary question on 11 September 2015 which showed that arrests by the Hawks had declined from 14 793 in 2010/11 to 5 847 in 2015.

Bob would apply for the remedial legislation to be declared

invalid, and the location of the Hawks in the SAPS to be rejected on circumstantial grounds. The HSF would also apply for the remedial legislation to be declared invalid, but would not contest the placement of the Hawks in the SAPS.

Given this overlap, the Western Cape High Court decided that both matters should be heard together. The deputy judge president awarded dates for an urgent hearing, and directed that the matter be heard by a full bench of three judges. A timetable was set for the exchange of affidavits in answer to the founding papers and replying papers. Dates were set for the exchange of heads of argument, and the parties set about addressing the tasks at hand before the hearing, scheduled for August 2013.

Unlike the previous case, the state decided that the president, minister of police and minister of justice should all be separately represented. Three teams of advocates were assembled to prepare and present their cases, and would almost certainly cost the taxpayer far more than previous state representation. Among other things, the representatives of the minister of police would ask the court to strike down much of the material adduced in relation to the circumstances of the executive, the SAPS and the Hawks in Bob's application.

Judges allocated to hear the matter were Judges Siraj Desai, André le Grange and Judith Cloete. Judge Desai had sat in the previous round, so he very fairly gave the parties an opportunity to ask him to recuse himself. Nobody asked, so he presided as the senior judge in the matter for the second time.

At some time in August, in the course of preparing argument, Bob's three advocates – Niel Taljaard of the East London Bar and Guy Lloyd-Roberts, a co-director of Accountability Now and former member of the Cape Bar and I – adjourned for lunch at the Kelvin Grove club in Newlands, Cape Town. Colin Eglin shuffled in with a newspaper under his arm, obviously intending to eat alone. I asked Niel and Guy whether they would like to meet a former leader of the opposition who had played a significant role in shaping the constitution we were invoking in our quest to improve the structure and functioning of the Hawks. They were both delighted by my suggestion.

I approached Eglin, and invited him to join us, if he was alone and prepared to postpone his engagement with his newspaper. The good politician, even in retirement, he graciously accepted the invitation, and joined our table for a plate of the famous lamb curry. We explained why we were working together, and it soon emerged that Eglin had lost none of his political acuity. With unerring accuracy, he pointed out that the problem was not legal but political, and would remain so until the political will necessary to address corruption could be mustered. At that time, we agreed, it did not seem to exist.

We moved on to a more general discussion in which I pointed to the achievements of Accountability Now, hoping to elicit a quotable comment. 'You haven't achieved much despite all the activity, have you?' Eglin said with a smile.

'Not as much as we would have liked,' I replied. 'Do you think we should give up?' 'No, no, no,' he retorted; 'keep on irritating them – it serves a very useful purpose.'

Encouraged by our chance meeting with such a legendary figure, we returned to our paperwork to find new ways of 'irritating them'. At that time, Eglin was 88 years old. He died soon afterwards, on 29 November 2013, two weeks before judgment was handed down.

The hearing was spread over five days in August, September and October. It did not start well for Team Glenister. The presiding judge asked us to open the batting for the applicants, and then went into a tirade against Bob for referring to corruption in high places in the course of going into 'the circumstances' relevant to legislation setting up the kind of anti-corruption machinery South Africa required. It clearly did not help that Judge Desai was a former ANC branch chairman, and that Zuma had been his client when he was a member of the Cape Bar.

Foaming at the mouth, Judge Desai took exception to Tony Yengeni being referred to as a convicted criminal. Yengeni is indeed a convicted criminal. He was convicted of defrauding parliament by not disclosing his accepting a luxury vehicle at an abnormal discount from a company involved in the arms deal while chairing the parliamentary committee meant to oversee the deal. Yengeni was carried shoulder-high to and from prison by his fans in the ANC. He had served in the ANC underground with Anwa Dramat, who was plucked from an obscure post in crime intelligence to head the Hawks.

Judge Desai was obviously irritated by these home truths in Bob's papers, and was determined that media representatives covering the opening arguments should be made aware of the extent of his displeasure. It did not help to point out that the Constitutional Court itself had indicated that parliament should attend to what was required 'in the circumstances', and that it was therefore perfectly in order to sketch the relevant circumstances, including the extent of corruption in and around the ANC government. Indeed, this was not even mentioned in the eventual judgment, which dealt harshly with Bob's evidence of the circumstances. Opposing counsel (very properly) tried to dissuade Judge Desai from making a punitive cost award against Bob in respect of this aspect of his case, but this gracious gesture did not succeed; the court did make a punitive award, which was later reduced to ordinary costs upon appeal.

The HSF argument presented by David Unterhalter SC to the full bench of the Western Cape High Court in August 2013 was received far more graciously than that of Team Glenister. The narrow scope of the points and the detailed technical analysis by a highly skilled team of advocates caused the court to consider the specifics of the law, and the shortcomings of the remedial legislation. It became clear that the amendments did not stand up to scrutiny.

The arguments presented by the three teams for the state led by Michael Donen SC for the minister of police, Renata Williams SC for the minister of justice, and Kemp J Kemp SC for the president did not make a significant dent in the case against the technical merits of the new legislation. Interestingly, the three government teams could not always agree on the technical interpretation of the law whose constitutionality they were defending. This confusion and contradiction merely served to illustrate the flaws in the scheme of the act: clearly, the government was bent on doing as little as possible to satisfy the criteria set by the Constitutional Court in Glenister II. The fact that this could not always be done in an intelligible and consistent fashion was exposed when the three teams for the executive branch of government could not come up with a consistent and coherent interpretation of the finer points of the law.

Argument ended in October 2013 with the replying arguments of the applicants in the two cases. Spread over five days in three months, the argument was a marathon, but the parties were not made to wait long for the judgment. Justice Cloete delivered it on Friday 13 December, the last day of the court term, on behalf of a unanimous bench.

The legislation was struck down as unconstitutional in a number of specific respects. More specifically, the judgment stated that certain sections of the SAPS Amendment Act of 2012 were inconsistent with the constitution, and invalid to the extent that they failed to make the DPCI sufficiently independent. The declaration of constitutional invalidity was suspended for 12 months to give parliament an opportunity to remedy the defects, and the orders were referred to the Constitutional Court for confirmation. The state parties were ordered to pay the costs of the HSF application. As noted earlier, the court granted an application by counsel for the minister of police to strike out Bob's evidence of the circumstances which ought to have informed the legislative decision making. He was ordered to pay the full costs of this aspect of the proceedings. Added to this, no costs were awarded to him in respect of the technical aspects of the legislation, despite the fact that this part of his case overlapped with that of the HSF.

The different parties now needed to respond in different ways. The HSF needed to apply to the Constitutional Court to confirm the relief granted, and appeal against the adverse rulings on other features of the legislation. The government representatives all decided, separately, to appeal against the High Court's findings in respect of the legislation, granting partial relief to the HSF. Bob, in turn, wanted to appeal against the adverse ruling in respect of his circumstantial evidence of corruption, the adverse cost award in respect of this ruling, and the refusal to grant him costs in respect of the rest. Besides this, he wanted to reapply for the entire Amendment Act to be declared unconstitutional.

All parties wanted a hearing in the Constitutional Court as soon as possible. Applications for leave to appeal, the application for the confirmation hearing and the papers opposing all applications were swiftly prepared, and a date for hearing was set down in May 2014. Due to an administrative glitch, the State Attorney failed to serve and file the president's argument, so when the parties assembled in the Constitutional Court, some were surprised to see counsel representing the president in court, as were members of the court themselves. The matter was clearly not ripe for hearing, and the president was ordered to pay the costs wasted by the postponement. The case would now be heard in August 2014.

The Glenister team was led by Izak Smuts SC of the Grahamstown Bar, assisted by Niel Taljaard and Guy Lloyd-Roberts. The other parties had the same legal teams as in the Cape. The false start in May was relegated to the past, and the matter was fully ventilated. The issues were neatly summarised in a media release issued by the court prior to argument, aimed at helping the media to report on the case, thus explaining it to the general public.

It said the Constitutional Court would hear applications for leave to appeal and for the confirmation of an order of the Western Cape Division of the High Court. The High Court had declared various sections of the SAPS Amendment Act of 2012 – which regulated the creation and operation of the state's anti-corruption entity, informally known as the Hawks – to be unconstitutional. The Amendment Act was intended to rectify the Constitutional Court's finding in Glenister II that the original legislation was invalid. Following a renewed challenge, the Western Cape High Court had declared that some of the remedial provisions were still unconstitutional, as they did not provide the Hawks with an adequate degree of independence.

In the current matter, the HSF and Glenister were again arguing that certain provisions of the SAPS Amendment Act failed to provide the Hawks with sufficient institutional and operational independence. Specific areas of concern included the possibility of undue political interference; a lack of parliamentary oversight; insufficient security of tenure; and inadequate dismissal procedures and appointment criteria.

The HSF was also appealing against the High Court's refusal to declare other provisions of the SAPS Amendment Act unconstitutional, and Glenister was also appealing against the entire High Court order on the basis that the whole scheme of the Act was unconstitutional. Alternatively, he aligned himself with the HSF submissions.

The state respondents opposed the confirmation of the order of invalidity, and were appealing against the High Court order. They argued, the media release concluded, that the SAPS Amendment Act created sufficient independence for the Hawks, and that the doctrine of the separation of powers prevented the courts from being overly prescriptive about the legislative measures taken by the state to fight corruption.

Argument was heard, and the bench grilled counsel in the usual way. The legal teams gathered for judgment on 27 November. Once again, the court had not reached a unanimous decision, and several judgments were delivered. To the surprise of many, the majority did something no one had asked for: it had 'edited' the remedial Hawks legislation in order to align it with the constitution. Everyone, including the Cape full bench, had expected the Constitutional Court to refer the legislation back to parliament, in the event of the applicants winning on any point. The court, in its majority judgment, did not regard this as necessary or even desirable. In effect, it rewrote the legislation in order to achieve a result consistent with the constitution.

Bob's argument, that the location of the Hawks within the police was unconstitutional 'in the circumstances', again received short shrift. As the majority were not prepared to consider expert testimony that locating the Hawks unit in the SAPS was incompatible with its independence and effectiveness, this was a foregone conclusion.

Subsequent events have shown that Bob was right in raising the red flag about locating the Hawks in the SAPS. On 23 December 2014, the minister of police, Nathi Nhleko, suspended General Anwa Dramat, head of the DPCI since its inception, pending a probe into his alleged involvement in the illegal rendition of four Zimbabweans in November 2010. In doing so, Nhleko seemed to follow the wording of the SAPS Amendment Act which had by then been struck down by the Constitutional Court. The HSF questioned the constitutionality of the move, but Dramat, reportedly in fear of his life and under family pressure, resigned rather than tough it out. His replacement, General Berning Ntlemeza, has an adverse High Court credibility and integrity finding against him.

Besides this, from early 2012 onwards, top figures in the SAPS and NPA made a series of widely publicised attempts to dislodge the Hawks boss in KwaZulu-Natal, General Johan Booysen. This did not speak well of the security of tenure of Hawks personnel.

However, when judgment was handed down in the last of the Glenister cases, all this was yet to come. Once again, Constitutional Court staff played an invaluable role in making sense of the complicated legal conclusions and warring judgments. In summary, the media release that emerged with the final judgment in Glenister III said the following:

The Constitutional Court had delivered judgment in two applications for leave to appeal against decisions of the Western Cape Division of the High Court, and an application for the confirmation of a High Court order. The matter concerned the independence of the anti-corruption unit in the SAPS.

The State's anti-corruption unit, the DPCI, informally known as the Hawks, was established in 2008. The Constitutional Court had previously identified various constitutional defects with the legislation introducing the DPCI in Glenister II. The SAPS Amendment Act of 2012 was enacted to cure these constitutional defects.

Following a renewed court challenge, the High Court had found that some of the provisions of the SAPS Amendment Act were still inconsistent with the constitutional obligation to create a structurally and operationally independent anti-corruption unit. The High Court also dismissed part of the HSF application to have several further provisions declared unconstitutional. In addition, the High Court struck out additional evidence Glenister had tried to lead, and dismissed his application to declare the entire legislative scheme of the DPCI constitutionally invalid.

In the Constitutional Court, the HSF had contended that various provisions which were not declared unconstitutional undermined the institutional and functional independence of the DPCI. Specific areas of concern included the renewability of terms of office; suspension and dismissal procedures; and appointment criteria of the national head of the DPCI, as well as possible undue interference by the minister of police via the implementation of policy guidelines governing the DPCI's jurisdiction.

Glenister had sought to have the entire SAPS Amendment Act declared unconstitutional. Alternatively, he aligned himself with the HSF's submissions. He also sought leave to appeal against the order of the High Court striking out large portions of his evidence.

The State parties had opposed the confirmation of the order of invalidity and all other applications. They contended that the SAPS Amendment Act insulated the DPCI against undue political interference, and that the doctrine of the separation of powers prevented the courts from being overly prescriptive about the legislative measures designed to fight corruption.

In the majority judgment, Chief Justice Mogoeng (with Deputy Chief Justice Moseneke, Justices Jafta, Khampepe, Zondo, and Acting Justice Leeuw concurring) dismissed Glenister's application for leave to appeal with costs; granted the HSF's application for leave to appeal; but dismissed the appeal against the High Court's refusal to declare certain sections unconstitutional, and confirmed the substantial part of the High Court's order.

Certain defects highlighted in Glenister II, the media release said, had not been cured. These included the unconstitutionality of the provisions relating to the extension of tenure of the national head of the DPCI; undue political interference in the operations of the DPCI through ministerial policy guidelines; and the untrammelled power of the minister of police to remove the head of the DPCI. The remedy employed by the Court was to sever those parts of specific sections that were found to be inconsistent with the constitutional obligation to create an anti-corruption unit that enjoyed adequate structural and operational independence.

In a separate judgment, Froneman J (with Cameron J concurring) agreed with the majority judgment, except for the finding that the process of appointing the national head was constitutionally compliant (in which respect he concurred with Cameron J); and its dismissal of Glenister's application for leave to appeal. He argued that Glenister II did not foreclose either the constitutional challenge to the SAPS Amendment Act as a whole, or the leading of additional evidence to sustain that challenge. In respect of Glenister's challenge to the SAPS Amendment Act, leave to appeal should be granted, but the order should ensure that the minister and the anti-corruption unit could coexist productively without resorting to the more drastic relief sought by Glenister. He would thus dismiss the appeal.

Madlanga J concurred with Froneman J except to the extent that Froneman J concurred with Cameron J. A separate judgment by Cameron J (with Froneman J and Van der Westhuizen J concurring) held that the process for appointing the national head was not constitutionally compliant. In his view, concentrating the power of appointment in a single member of the Cabinet, without express parliamentary approval, would jeopardise the DPCI's independence. He disagreed with Mogoeng CJ that Glenister II prevented the Court from making this finding, and would therefore confirm the High Court order declaring this section invalid.

In a separate judgment, Nkabinde J concurred with the main judgment, but found that the section of the Amendment Act empowering the minister of police to prescribe measures for testing the integrity of DPCI members was unconstitutional. In her view, the empowering provision failed to list the factors necessary to guide the exercise of the discretionary power, and to inform those adversely affected by the exercise of that power under what circumstances they could seek relief.

Finally, Van der Westhuizen J agreed with Mogoeng C J except for the following points: Firstly, he agreed with Cameron J that parliament should be involved in appointing the national head of the DPCI. Secondly, he aligned himself in part with Froneman J's judgment by concluding that Glenister's application for leave to appeal should have been granted, and certain parts of his evidence should not have been struck out. He was uncomfortable with the majority's labelling of this evidence as 'political posturing', and found that this did not provide legitimate grounds for striking out evidence. No legal scheme could successfully rule out all corruption. This could only be achieved if those in decision-making positions had integrity, and were committed to the values embodied in the Constitution.

The amendments drafted by the Constitutional Court immediately passed into law. However, the executive simply appeared to ignore these amendments, notably in the course of suspending Dramat, which – according to the latest legislation – could only be done by parliament.

The HSF continued to fight the good fight, building on its contribution during Glenister II and III, by contesting Dramat's dismissal, and the appointment of Ntlemeza as his successor. However, the fight against corruption was inevitably weakened by the location of the Hawks within the police.

Having taken up the fight in December 2007, Bob had now reached the point where he felt the campaign for effective anti-corruption machinery had to be waged in the political rather than the legal arena.

Accountability Now continued to campaign for a new Chapter Nine institution, the Integrity Commission. The constitution would have to be amended to achieve the situation in which the work of the Auditor General and Public Protector was complemented and supplemented by an institution that could, we suggested, be called the Eagles. Amending the constitution would require the support of two thirds of the members of the National Assembly.

Creating the political will to garner this amount of support among politicians, who included numerous prominent beneficiaries of corruption, would entail a sea change in the outlook of those elected to represent South Africa's citizens in parliament. At the time of writing, neither our judges nor politicians seemed to have the appetite to establish such an institution.

If this lack of will were to persist, one final avenue seemed open, either to Bob Glenister or any other person prepared to take up the cudgels on behalf of clean administration and good governance. In Glenister II, the court required that the parliamentary efforts at remedial legislation should be aimed at arriving at the decision of a reasonable decision-maker 'in the circumstances'. Precisely what this meant was the subject of some debate and conflicting reasoning in the judgments handed down in Glenister III. The majority of the court regarded Bob's reliance upon the sorry state of affairs in the executive, the ministry of police, the police service itself and the Hawks as 'odious political posturing' which they therefore disallowed as admissible evidence. The minority were prepared to have regard to these 'circumstances', but did not regard them as serious enough to justify moving the anti-corruption unit out of the police.

If it could be shown that Bob's concerns about the state of affairs in the above-mentioned institutions of state were justified, and that they had all deteriorated further, a case could be made for asking the Constitutional Court to revise its judgment in Glenister III.

Should this be attempted, it would be possible to refer to the removal of General Anwa Dramat as leader of the Hawks, and his pending trial on charges of kidnapping. The irregular way in which he was suspended by the minister of police could also be highlighted, with reference to the litigation launched by the HSF when this occurred. The way in which his successor was appointed was also the subject of ongoing litigation, whose outcome could provide further fodder for Glenister IV, if Bob could be persuaded to return to the highest court in the land for an unprecedented fourth time.

Other elements could be used in support of a claim for an independent Integrity Commission. The steadily deteriorating productivity of the Hawks, as measured in terms of arrests year on year, was an indictment of their effectiveness and efficiency. Their preoccupation with matters as diverse as counter-terrorism measures and rhino poaching also demonstrated a lack of specialisation and the concentrated focus that would come with true compliance with the STIRS criteria, particularly that of specialisation. A unit that was not dedicated to combating corruption could not comply with the characteristics of an effective anti-corruption unit as prescribed in the judgment in Glenister II.

The persistent campaign to remove General Johan Booysen from his job as head of the Hawks in Durban was a matter of some concern to those who sought clean administration. His skirmishes in the courts could be used to illustrate that members of the Hawks lacked security of tenure of office, and that the executive was intolerant of officers willing to investigate corruption in high places. The problems surrounding General Booysen had arisen because he was prepared to investigate persons who were close to the centre of power in his province and elsewhere in the country.

Other officers in the Hawks had also been given a torrid time. Some might be able to show that their independent mode of operation, and their willingness to investigate the 'big fish', was the true reason for the disciplinary actions taken against them. This would, as with Booysen, impact deleteriously on their independence and security of tenure of office.

At the time of writing, the South African Police Union was calling for a commission of inquiry into the actions of the minister of police in respect of the employment of convicted criminals in the crime intelligence division of the SAPS. If the allegations against the minister were true, they were serious, and would certainly justify an argument that control over the anti-corruption unit should be transferred to parliament, and away from the cabinet. The prospects of a more even-handed outcome would be greatly enhanced by parliament's multi-party nature. Nefarious elements could not capture the state as easily if the Hawks were to answer to parliament and not to the minister of police.

The Constitutional Court would have to be persuaded that it had erred in allowing the Hawks to remain in the police. This was not necessarily an insurmountable obstacle. All that was required was for a solid case to be built on the basis of the facts available when the matter went to court. The fate of the litigation about the leadership of the Hawks, involving Ntlemeza as well as Booysen, the outcome of legal challenges surrounding the 'resignation' of Mxolisi Nxasana in June 2015 as national director of public prosecutions, and the response to the alleged irregularities on the part of the minister could all help to persuade the Constitutional Court to reconsider its majority judgment in Glenister III.

The Nxasana matter was of particular interest. On Sunday 31 May 2015, the Presidency issued a brief statement noting that

President Zuma had reached a settlement with Nxasana in terms of which he would vacate his position as national director of public prosecutions on 1 June. No reasons were provided.

Puzzlingly, it added: 'The government recognises that Mr Nxasana is professionally competent and possesses the requisite experience and integrity required to hold a senior position.' The details of the settlement were also not disclosed, but it eventually emerged that this comprised the undiscounted unexpired value of Nxasana's term of office, amounting to more than R17 million.

By June 2016, when this book went to press, this peculiar arrangement and chain of events had become the subject matter of a criminal investigation of charges of corruption and defeating the ends of justice against the president and his minister of justice brought by Accountability Now. It had also become the subject matter of civil proceedings aimed at invalidating the settlement and resignation, brought by Freedom Under Law and Corruption Watch. The result of the civil proceedings would inform the progress of the criminal complaint.

Chapter 10

Breaking the bread cartel

———•———

*'Cast your bread upon the waters, for you will find it
after many days.'*
– Ecclesiasticus 11.1

ACTING JUDGES in South Africa's High Courts are an en-
dangered species. They are usually drawn from the ranks of
seasoned practitioners and senior magistrates, with a sprinkling
of legal academics, and are required to do the 'heavy lifting' in
the division in which they are appointed. Cynics often observe
that accepting an acting appointment is an act of insolvency for
senior practitioners, as their incomes from their practices usually far exceed the stipends paid to acting judges.

In theory, acting judges take the place of a permanent judge
who is on long leave, absent on business (such as a commission
of inquiry), or ill. In practice, the less attractive trials, the appeals with long records, and the bulkier paper-based motion
cases – especially those wrapped in legal arguments made of
razor-wire – are allocated to acting judges in disproportionate
dollops. Judges-president regard this practice as a baptism of
fire, or, in some instances, aversion therapy, designed to put the
hapless acting judges off a career on the bench for all time.
While many acting judges take up their appointments as a 'duty

call' in the sense of paying back the system for the privileges it has bestowed on them, most have to be cajoled into acting, even though a stint on the bench amounts to a nice break from the hurly-burly of legal practice.

In November 2010, Francois van Zyl SC, a senior and respected member of the Cape Bar, was serving as an acting judge in his home division. A former attorney-general in the 'homeland' of Transkei, with a background in the prosecution service of the old South Africa, he found himself on the bench for a spell, doing his civic duty in the motion court set aside for unopposed and urgent matters.

The Western Cape Division of the High Court – or Western Cape High Court, for short – has a refined view of what's urgent and what isn't. As a result, it has developed the notion of 'semi-urgency' for the purpose of giving deserving litigants an accelerated hearing, in a way that does not unduly prejudice those waiting their turn on the ordinary court rolls. As one of the duty judges of the week, Acting Judge Van Zyl found himself at the receiving end of two complex and novel applications that were alleged to be urgent – not just semi-urgent, because, the applicants said, the claims were on the point of becoming prescribed. The cases had to be heard and an order given in a matter of days. To his credit, Acting Judge Van Zyl heard the cases and made his orders within the time frame desired. This is hardly the optimum situation for an acting judge to find himself in, especially in circumstances in which all three respondents in the cases opposed the granting of relief with might and mane, using large teams of experienced lawyers.

The facts were relatively simple. Three bread producers –

Pioneer Foods, Tiger Consumer Brands and Premier Foods – had put their heads together to collude in three ways. First, they agreed to fix their bread price increases; second, they reduced the commissions payable to their respective distributors; and third, they agreed not to poach distributors from each other. This is classically how a cartel operates. As in many other countries, it is illegal to operate a cartel in South Africa. This one was swiftly reported to the Competition Commission by anguished bread distributors who found themselves with less commission for the same work. The Commission duly investigated the matter, and fined the participants heavily for their respective roles in the cartel, once its workings had been exposed with the help of the whistle-blowers.

This finding of cartel activity put consumers of bread and the distributors employed by the three bread manufacturers in a position to sue for damages. The novelty of the matter was that the applicants in the two cases (one on behalf of consumers, and the other on behalf of distributors) wanted to have a class action certified in each case, something that had not been done before in South Africa.

Initially the bread distributors, led by a doughty bread distributor and community activist called Imraahn Mukaddam, sought the advice of Charles Abrahams, a Cape-based attorney specialising in public interest litigation. They were about 100 in number, and had stories to tell in relation to the adverse, and in some cases fatal, impact of the cartel on their businesses.

It soon became apparent from the antecedent proceedings in the Competition Tribunal that the largest loss had been borne by consumers of bread sold at cartel prices. As a result,

Mukaddam and his team decided to attempt a class action for the hard-pressed consumers of bread as well. The Children's Resources Centre, a charitable trust, expressed interest in the matter, and joined the fray as an applicant.

The constitution does contemplate a procedure, of the kind pressed before Acting Judge Van Zyl, for infringements or threatened infringements of a right in the Bill of Rights. In such a situation, anyone acting as a member of or in the interests of a group or class of people may approach a competent court for appropriate relief. In 1998, the South African Law Reform Commission recommended to government that legislation be passed to facilitate class actions in South Africa. Seeing this proposed legislation as a potential rod for its own chastisement, the government shelved the draft bill, and left it to the courts to work out how best to deal with the class action suits so beloved of American jurisprudence.

This challenge was taken up in a case entitled *Permanent Secretary, Department of Welfare, Eastern Cape Provincial Government versus Ngxuza and others (2001)*. In 1997, the Eastern Cape provincial government decided to deal with the problem of 'ghost pensioners' by suspending various social grants, including disability grants, and requiring bona fide beneficiaries to reapply. However, the province lacked the resources to administer this process, leading to lengthy delays in restoring the benefits of many poor and disadvantaged people.

Eventually, the Legal Resources Centre (LRC) decided to institute a class action – via M N Ngxuza and others – on behalf of all recipients of disability grants in the province. In a judgment handed down in the Eastern Cape High Court in 2001,

Judge Johan Froneman (who was later appointed to the Constitutional Court) gave them permission to proceed with a class action, and ordered the provincial government to provide the LRC with all its records of grant beneficiaries eligible for class membership. For reasons best known to its managers, the provincial government appealed against the judgment.

In a landmark judgment handed down later in 2001, the Supreme Court of Appeal upheld the Froneman judgment, confirming the use of class actions in South Africa to combat infringements of constitutional rights. Among other things, the Supreme Court of Appeal used the legal rules utilised in the United States for deciding whether the group in question had been adequately defined, thereby effectively ruling that those rules would apply in South Africa as well.

These state that one or more members of a class may initiate legal action on behalf of all other members if the class is so large that it is impractical for all its members to undertake joint legal action; there are questions of law or fact common to the class; the claims or defence of the representative parties are typical or the claims or defence of the class are similar; and the representative parties would fairly and adequately protect the interests of the class. These four requirements are commonly known as: 'numerosity', 'commonality', 'typicality', and 'adequacy of representation'. However, the Supreme Court of Appeal reiterated that this could only be done where a constitutional right had been infringed or threatened.

The Eastern Cape government also collected the sharp edge of the Appeal Court's tongue. Referring to its sustained efforts to oppose a class action, the judgment stated: 'All this speaks of a contempt for people and process that does not befit an organ of government under our constitutional dispensation. It is not the function of the courts to criticise government's decisions in the area of social policy. But when an organ of government invokes legal processes to impede the rightful claims of its citizens, it not only defies the Constitution, which commands all organs of state to be loyal to the Constitution, and requires that public administration be conducted on the basis that "people's needs must be responded to". It also misuses the mechanisms of the law, which it is the responsibility of the courts to safeguard.

'The province's approach to these proceedings was contradictory, cynical, expedient and obstructionist. It conducted the case as though it was at war with its own citizens, the more shamefully because those it was combating were in terms of secular hierarchies and affluence and power the least in its sphere. We were told, in extenuation, that unentitled claimants were costing the province R65 million per month. That misses the point, which is the cost the province's remedy exacted in human suffering on those who were entitled to benefits . . . '

But back to our story. The Ngxuza judgments seemed to open the door for class action claims by bread distributors as well as consumers. As each consumer had a relatively modest claim for the overpriced bread bought, a class action seemed the ideal vehicle for a consolidated action on behalf of consumers on the grounds that two human rights underwritten in the constitution – sufficient food for everyone, and basic nutrition for children – had been infringed or threatened.

In the case of the distributors, it was a bit more difficult to discern a human rights infringement. While section 22 of the Bill of Rights states that 'every citizen has the right to choose their trade, occupation or profession freely', it is a bit of a stretch to mould this right into a foundation for a damages action based on loss of income due to cartel activities of which the bread distribution businesses were victim.

Essentially, a class action occurs when a party or parties embark on legal action – typically claiming damages – on behalf of a larger group of people whom they claim to represent. Other members do not play a role in initiating the case, and do not appear in court, but are given an opportunity to indicate whether or not they would like to belong to the class in question. If the class action succeeds, all members are meant to benefit.

Class actions are most useful when the allegations involve a large number of people who have been wronged in the same way. Instead of each injured person bringing their own lawsuit, the class action allows the claims of all class members to be resolved in a single proceeding.

Class actions developed in the United States, and are still most common in that country, adding to its reputation for excessive litigation. But they are spreading to other countries too, notably to allow consumer organisations to bring claims on behalf of consumers. As noted earlier, the constitution has opened the door to class actions in South Africa, and South African judges have thus far drawn on the American approach in developing local jurisprudence.

In American class actions, at least one of the parties, whether the plaintiffs or defendants, are collectively represented by a member or members of the group in question. Those members, known as the 'named' plaintiffs or defendants, are present in court, and litigate on behalf of themselves and the absent class members.

Class actions are initiated by filing a proposed or 'putative' action in terms of which the potential claimants seek to represent themselves and other parties. To proceed, they must satisfy certain requirements. Until this happens, the class is referred to as a 'putative' or 'potential' class, and its members as 'putative' or 'potential' class members.

First, potential claimants must define the class they seek to represent. This must be precise enough to allow the court to determine who belongs to the class and who doesn't.

Second, they must be members of the class they seek to represent, and must have relevant 'standing' to assert their claims.

Third, classes must meet four criteria spelled out in the American legal rules referred to earlier, widely referred to as numerosity, commonality, typicality, and adequacy of representation. Potential class actions must also satisfy at least one of the following three requirements:

- separate actions could establish inconsistent standards of conduct, or substantially impair other class members' ability to protect their interests;
- joint relief would be appropriate because the party opposing the class acted on grounds that are generally applicable to the entire class; and
- Common issues of law and fact predominate over individual issues, and a class action is the best way of resolving the

plaintiffs' claims. In actions for monetary damages, this is regarded as the most important requirement.

Courts determine before a trial whether the potential claimants meet these requirements. If they do, the class is certified, and the class action proceeds. If they don't, the action fails, and claimants are left to pursue their claims individually.

Today, most American class actions are initiated on an 'opt-out' rather than an 'opt-in' basis. This means that all putative class members are assumed to be part of a class unless they give notice that they wish to opt out. By contrast, 'opt-in' class actions mean that all putative class members who wish to be regarded as members, and benefit from any awards, need to give notice that they wish to opt in.

If the court certifies the class in question, it will set specific deadlines for the representative plaintiffs to notify absent class members, and for absent members to decide whether they wish to opt in or out. The notices, and their intended distribution, have to be approved by the court. Notice is usually given either by mail, if this is practicable, or via the media.

Given all this, it was clear that the cases for bread consumers and distributors differed in several important respects, and required different approaches. Specifically, given the differences in extent of the two proposed classes, the opt-in model seemed more appropriate in one instance, and the opt-out model in the other. For these and other reasons, Mukaddam and his team decided to pursue these matters separately, with one application brought on behalf of the distributors, and the other on behalf of consumers. Acting Judge Van Zyl heard and pronounced on both at the same time.

The consumer case was brought by nine applicants: the Children's Resource Centre (CRC) Trust, the Black Sash Trust, Cosatu, the National Consumer Forum, and five individuals representing a spread of bread consumers. The first applicant was represented by its co-ordinator, Marcus Chinasamy Solomon. The respondents were the three bread producers found guilty of collusive practices, namely Pioneer Foods, Tiger Consumer Brands and Premier Foods.

In a founding affidavit, Solomon said the Competition Commission had instituted an investigation into the conduct of the respondents. It found they had engaged in 'restricted horizontal practice' by acting in concert to fix the selling price of bread in the Western Cape, and dividing markets. This unlawful conduct had breached the rights of both bread consumers and bread distributors.

The applicants intended to institute a class action against the respondents on behalf of consumers for compensation and related relief. To this end, they would seek leave to represent the class, as well as ancillary relief about the procedures to be followed.

On the suitability of class actions, the affidavit said affected consumers constituted a large number of people, running into millions. Given their socio-economic circumstances, and the costs of litigation, most did not have the financial means and resources to embark on litigation. Also, individual claims were too small in value to justify individual action, but taken together amounted to a large amount of money.

The respondents were the three largest bread producers, which dominated the market in the Western Cape. Together, they produced bread that was bought and consumed by millions of consumers on a daily basis. Every consumer who had bought their products during the period in question had suffered damages as a result of the unlawful price fixing and other prohibited practices.

Relief sought in the class action would take two forms. First, calculating the damages that consumers had suffered would require access to the respondents' records and accounts. As a result, the applicants would seek access to the accounts in order to establish the damages suffered by the class.

Second, the damages suffered by each bread consumer were very small. If global damages were awarded, the cost of distributing it to consumers would be prohibitive. Moreover, it would be difficult or impossible to establish precisely how much of the respondents' bread each consumer had bought during the period in question. For this reason, the applicants would seek an order that would require the respondents to pay the unlawful overcharge into a trust or trusts to be established for the benefit of consumers.

On the appropriateness of a class action, the affidavit argued that millions of bread consumers in the Western Cape had been affected by the respondents' unlawful conduct, and that a class action was the only practical and efficient way of resolving their claims.

The affidavit defined the proposed class as consisting of all consumers of bread in the Western Cape who were affected by the unlawful conduct of the respondents. For practical purposes, it said, this 'virtually amounted to the public at large in the Western Cape'. (This later led to a moment of dry humour in the courtroom when Acting Judge Van Zyl asked counsel for the applicants whether he should recuse himself as, in terms of this definition, he was also a putative member of the class in question.)

On the issue of class membership, the affidavit said it was not practical or in the interests of justice to require that individual consumers opt into the class action. The class was very large, the individual claims were very small, and many members of the class did not have the knowledge of their rights and access to the information and advice that would enable them to make the decision to opt into the class. Under these circumstances, consumers should be given the option to opt out of the class.

Proposed steps to publicise giving consumers notice of the class action included notices in five newspapers, in several languages, and broadcasts on five radio stations, again in several languages. Moreover the, court should order the respondents to place sticky labels on all their products, advising consumers of the class action.

On the issue of leave to represent the class, the affidavit said the constitution provided for class actions if a right in the Bill of Rights had been infringed or threatened. In this instance, the applicants would indeed allege that rights in the Bill of Right had been infringed.

Bread was the staple diet of many South Africans. A large number of South Africans – up to 50 per cent – lived in poverty. For such people, a small increase in the bread price, which they paid on a daily basis, could have a material impact on their ability to obtain sufficient food for themselves and their families.

The constitution provided that everyone had the right to access to sufficient food, and also that every child had the right to basic nutrition. This placed a negative obligation on persons such as the respondents to desist from preventing or impairing the right of access to sufficient food, and children's rights to basic nutrition.

On the issue of class representation, the CRC had a direct interest in the matter, and was a suitable person to represent the class. It had been established 27 years previously with the aim of assisting children to participate in educational, health and nutritional projects. In the course of it work, it had found that bread constituted an essential part of the diet of children, and in some instances the primary source of their diet. In September 2002, the Centre had begun to engage the national government on the issue of increasing poverty and the high rate of malnutrition among children.

Research had shown that malnutrition remained a major problem. Stunting through malnutrition affected one in every five children, and is known to have a significant and adverse impact on the physical and emotional development of the children as well as their scholastic performance.

The Centre had become particularly concerned when it became known that the respondents had colluded in the fixing of the bread price. It believed that such conduct on the part of the respondents had directly and substantially contributed to bread becoming less accessible to children. The Centre had no interest of its own in the class action, beyond the public interest goals which it sought to promote. Similar arguments were offered in respect of the other applicants. Lastly, the affidavit argued that the applicants' attorneys and counsel were suitably qualified and experienced to represent the class.

The applicants initially restricted their claims to the Western Cape as they believed claims elsewhere would fall outside the jurisdiction of the Western Cape High Court, and similar applications would need to be brought in Gauteng. When, in the course of the court hearing, it emerged that this was unnecessary, they extended the scope of the claim to the entire country.

The application for a class action on behalf of bread distributors was launched by Mukaddam, described as a bread distributor based in Elsies River in the Western Cape; W E M Distributors CC, a bread distributing company based in Wellington; and Abdul Kariem Ebrahim, a bread distributor based in Belhar. In this instance, the applicants sought to institute a class action against the respondents on behalf of about 100 bread distributors in the Western Cape. In a founding affidavit, Mukaddam argued that distributors had suffered substantial damages. Many had been forced to close their businesses, and others faced sequestration. Given this, many could not afford individual litigation, and a class action was therefore the only effective means of obtaining effective relief.

While largely replicating the consumer application, this application differed from it in two major ways. First, it proposed the establishment of an opt-in class. Unlike consumers, the applicants argued, the class of distributors was relatively small, and easily identifiable from records held by the respondents. All distributors would be given proper and adequate notice, and an opportunity to opt into the class. Once respondents' records had been accessed, damages could be easily calculated.

Notices would be placed in several newspapers and broadcast on several radio stations. Moreover, the respondents should be ordered to send written notices to all distributors by prepaid registered post.

Second, as regards the issue of constitutional rights, the applicants argued that distributors were also directly affected by the respondents' conduct that had impaired the right of access to sufficient food, and children's rights to basic nutrition. It had also infringed their right to freely choose their trade, occupation and profession, provided in section 22 of the constitution.

As noted previously, Acting Judge Van Zyl was obliged to hear argument about all this as a matter of urgency, which he did over two days in between all the other cases on his roll. He had also to prepare an order within a few days in order to prevent the alleged lapse of the proposed claims before summons could be issued pursuant to the certification of a class action. He did so via a 10 000-word judgment, which must have kept him up into the early hours.

Addressing the issue of class action in general prior to addressing the two applications, Acting Judge Van Zyl noted that the 1996 constitution provided for class action when rights in the Bill of Rights had been infringed or threatened. In *Ngxuza versus the Department of Welfare*, Judge Froneman had found that practical difficulties that could arise in class actions could not justify their denial, when the constitution made specific provision for this.

Judge Froneman had dealt with the practical objections to class actions, including the objection that the courts would be engulfed by interfering busy-bodies rushing to court for spurious reasons – the so-called 'floodgates' argument – and the objection that the common interest of applicants and those they sought to represent would often be broad and vague – the so-called 'classification' difficulty.

In respect of the 'floodgates' objection, Judge Froneman had noted that unjustified litigation could be curtailed by requiring that leave must be sought from the High Court to proceed on a representative basis prior to actually embarking on that road. The 'classification' problem could be addressed in the same way at a preliminary stage. The determination of a common interest sufficient to justify class, group, or representative representation would depend on the facts of each case. The common interest had to relate to the alleged infringement of a fundamental right, as required by the constitution.

The Ngxuza judgment had been upheld on appeal. Dealing with the respondent's argument that the class in that matter was not adequately defined, the Supreme Court of Appeal had confirmed that a class action had to comply with the following criteria: the class should be so numerous that joinder of all its members was impracticable; there were questions of law and fact common to the class; the claims of the applicants representing the class were typical of the claims of the rest; and the applicants would fairly and adequately protect the interests of the class. The Supreme Court of Appeal had concluded that the requisites for a class action were present.

The provisions for class actions in the constitution only applied directly to infringements of or threats to rights in the Bill of Rights. However, in a paper published in 1998, the South

African Law Commission had concluded that the scope of class actions should be broadened to non-Bill of Rights cases as well. Moreover, while the Ngxuza matter had only involved a Bill of Rights issue, the judgment indicated that a class action not limited to Bill of Rights cases should be available in South African law.

Like Judge Froneman, the Law Commission report had recommended that a preliminary application should be brought, requesting leave to institute a class action and to ask for directions in respect of procedure. This would prevent potential abuse of the process; shield defendants against unreasonable burden of complex and costly litigation; protect the interest of absent class members.

The Law Commission had also spelled out criteria for judging applications for the certification of class actions. These were that the application should involve an identifiable class of people; that a common cause of action was disclosed; that there were issues of fact or law which were common to the class; a suitable representative was available; the interests of justice would be served; and a class action was the most appropriate way of dealing with the matter in question. Acting Judge Van Zyl said he would follow the Law Commission's recommendations in dealing with both applications.

In the event, the consumer case fell foul of two of these criteria: class identification, and a common cause of action. On the first score, Acting Judge Van Zyl noted that the applicants had described the class as all consumers who were prejudicially affected by bread prices as a result of the respondents' unlawful actions. This included corporate entities such as companies operating hotels, restaurants and the like, as well as millions of others whose constitutional rights had not 'by any stretch of the imagination' been threatened or infringed.

This raised the issue of whether class actions should be available in non-Bill of Rights matters. He would accept that the applicants could bring a class action for damages, and that the description of the broad class of consumers was sufficient to identify those who might have a potential claim. However, the applicants had failed to identify the period or periods during which the damages claim had arisen. Therefore, as in the case of the narrower class, the parameters of the intended damages action were not sufficiently defined so as to identify all the people who would be bound by the result.

As regards a cause of action, the applicants had asked the court to order the respondents to provide accounts of the excessive charges; order the establishment of a trust or trusts which would receive the damages, and use them to promote the interests of the class; and order the respondents to pay damages to the trust. However, the respondents did not supply bread directly to consumers, but to the retail trade and bread distributors, and were therefore not contractually obliged to render accounts to consumers. The respondents also did not have a statutory duty to do so, and there was no fiduciary relationship between the respondents and consumers that obliged the former to account to the latter. Accordingly, the consumers had no right to demand that the respondents render such accounts to them, and for such accounts to be debated.

In light of the applicants' failure to sufficiently identify the class they wished to represent, and to disclose a cause of action, the consumer applications stood to be dismissed. Given that the applicants intended to promote the advancement of constitutional justice, he would not order them to pay the respondents' costs.

As regards the distributor application, Acting Judge Van Zyl noted that section 22 of the constitution protected individuals rather than juristic persons. It followed that a juristic entity such as the second applicant, and many other prospective plaintiffs, could not claim protection under section 22. Again, he would accept that the applicants were able in principle to represent a class in non-Bill of Rights matters. However, he was not convinced that the issues of fact and law to be decided in respect of the various distributors and the respondents with whom they had dealt were such that the matter should be dealt with as a class action against the three respondents. For these reasons, the applicants had not made out a case for leave to institute a class action on behalf of the distributors. In this instance, Acting Judge Van Zyl ordered the applicants to pay the respondents' costs.

It was at this point that Accountability Now was approached in relation to this matter. It seemed ripe for appeal; however, the cartel members had argued that there was a potential conflict of interest between the consumers and distributors, especially if the distributors had simply recovered their reduced mark-ups from consumers. Rather than find themselves embroiled in arguments about the alleged conflict, the attorneys in the matter wisely decided to seek separate legal representation for the consumers and distributors.

Charles Abrahams, the senior attorney involved in the case,

who was also Terry Crawford-Browne's attorney in the arms deals case, phoned me on a Saturday afternoon. 'Paul, this case needs the Hoffman touch,' he pleaded. 'We've come unstuck so far, but the justice of the cause is very important to us as we want to start a silicosis class action for retired miners.'

I wondered aloud whether any human rights of bread distributors had been infringed, but Charles was adamant that section 22 was open to an interpretation that would assist the certification of the class. Cautiously, I said: 'Send us the judgment so we can consider the prospects of success on appeal.'

'We will find a firm of attorneys willing to act on contingency in the matter, and you will get a brief from them,' Charles replied, with audible relief.

Soon the judgment arrived from Terence Matzdorff, the senior attorney in the Cape Town branch of the Johannesburg firm Knowles, Hussain and Lindsay. I was pleased to be working with him as we had often collaborated during my years at the Cape Bar.

Chris Shone, a co-director of Accountability Now and an ace internet researcher, showed interest in being my junior in the matter. The first task at hand was to see what could be done to get permission from Acting Judge Van Zyl to appeal against his decision. This involves an application for leave to appeal that would need to demonstrate that another court might come to a different conclusion.

Fortunately for us, the team representing the bread consumers who were briefed by Charles from the get-go were in the same boat as us, and had definite ideas about how to persuade Acting Judge Van Zyl to grant leave to appeal to the Supreme

Court of Appeal in Bloemfontein. Geoff Budlender SC of the Cape Bar led the charge in the application for leave to appeal on behalf of the consumers, while Chris Shone, Peter Hazell SC and I appeared for the distributors duly briefed by Terence Matzdorff.

It was clear to us that it would take a lot of effort to persuade the acting judge to accept that another court might come to a different conclusion. He had obviously put considerable research and thought into the judgment, had dealt with the arguments raised in a very thorough way, and his reasoning was lucid and persuasive.

In part because the acting appointment of the judge had ended, and in part because of the difficulty of assembling such a large number of counsel, the argument in the application for leave to appeal was heard on a Saturday. To the chagrin of the rugby fans in court, the argument dragged on well past the scheduled time for the kick-off of an enticing Super Rugby fixture. The judge wanted to be sure that he had a full grasp on the criticisms of his judgment offered by the applicants and of the defences of his reasoning put up by the respondents, whose counsel doggedly defended the reasoning adopted by the court.

After considering the arguments for some weeks, the verdict was delivered. Leave to appeal was refused; the acting judge was not budging, and did not believe that there was a reasonable possibility of any other court coming to a different conclusion.

Chapter 11

The bread cartel goes to Bloemfontein . . . and Braamfontein

---·|·---

'Class struggles seem to have metamorphosed into class actions . . . People drawn together by social or material predicament, culture, race, sexual preference, residential proximity, faith and habits of consumption become legal persons as their common plaints turn them into plaintiffs with communal identities against the antagonists who allegedly have acted illegally against them.'

— John and Jean Comaroff

FOLLOWING THE rejection of leave to appeal in the Western Cape High Court, it was 'do or die' time for the applicants. The obvious avenue open to them was to petition the Supreme Court of Appeal in Bloemfontein for leave to appeal. Accountability Now's legal team considered the prospects of success in respect of the bread distributors, and stated our view in a memorandum. They weren't positive.

Key issues emanating from the Cape judgment, we noted, were the applicability of section 22 of the Constitution, and the commonality of the claims. Success would require a favourable finding in respect of both. While we might persuade another court to reach a different view in respect of the former issue, this was not the case in respect of the latter, in our view.

The fact that further litigation would run the risk of another adverse costs order also had to be considered. As matters stood, the applicants already had a costs order against them, with significant consequences. These would worsen if the petition did not succeed. In the circumstances, we believed petitioning the Supreme Court of Appeal for leave to appeal was ill-advised.

Fortunately, our client, the remarkable Imraahn Mukaddam, did not take our advice, partly because the adverse costs award by Acting Judge Van Zyl was set to ruin him and his co-applicants. The litigation dice had to be rolled once again, if for no other reason than to reverse the costs award. Once the distributors were in there and fighting over the costs award, there was no point in omitting the other aspects of Acting Judge Van Zyl's ruling.

Both applications for leave to appeal were prepared, and it was agreed between the parties that the appeals would be heard together in the event of leave being granted. Much to the surprise of their counsel, the Supreme Court of Appeal gave the distributors an opportunity to present argument attacking the adverse findings against them in the Western Cape High Court. The bread producers retained their previous teams for the appeal. The consumers briefed Willem van der Linde SC to lead their team in the absence of Geoff Budlender SC, who was otherwise engaged. In a nice touch, his son, Stephen, acted as junior counsel for the consumers.

The court, an imposing array of five judges presided over by Judge of Appeal Robert Nugent, directed that we bat first for the distributors on the opening day of argument, with the consumer case to follow on the second day. Soon after starting my argument, Judge Nugent objected that a camera operator behind me was distracting him. The operator, who was shooting video footage for a documentary to be called *Crumbs*, moved to a less obtrusive position, and the argument got under way. However, his presence facilitated a congenial hearing, as it kept everyone in court on their best behaviour.

It soon became apparent that the judges of appeal were not particularly impressed with the distributors' case. I was peppered with questions about the definition of the class or classes we wanted to have certified, the availability of a joint or multi-claimant action for the limited number of distributors of bread involved in the case, and the absence of exceptional circumstances justifying the proposed class certification. However, the judges seemed comfortable with the idea that a general class action – in other words, one not limited to human rights infringements – had a place in modern South African jurisprudence, and should be developed by the courts in the absence of legislation of the kind suggested by the Law Commission in 1998.

On the second day, we were spectators as the consumers took their turn to present their case. The court had great difficulty with the notion that the losses of individual consumers of bread should be paid into a trust for the benefit of hungry children, and a heated court debate ensued. The judgments were not long in coming.

'When may a class action be brought, and what procedural requirements must be satisfied before it is instituted? These two questions confront this court in litigation arising from an investigation by the Competition Commission into the bread producing industry, initially in the Western Cape, and later in four other provinces in South Africa . . . '

With these magisterial words, Judge Malcolm Wallis started his judgment. Seemingly not prepared to be outdone by Acting Judge Van Zyl in quantitative terms, he then set out to answer these questions in a 22 000-word ruling, with Judges Nugent, Ponnan, Malan and Tshiqi concurring. After working his way through the factual background, the High Court proceedings and the legal issues, Judge Wallis spelled out the requirements and criteria for competent class actions in considerable detail before circling back to the matter at hand.

Measured against these principles, he concluded that the appellants' claim was 'not legally untenable'. The class had been defined too broadly, but there were grounds for believing that it could be defined more precisely. The relief the appellants wished to claim was also not competent. However, in the light of the principles laid down in this judgment, appropriate relief could probably be formulated.

He had 'considerable sympathy' for the learned acting judge who had been confronted with an extremely urgent application, and had to wrestle with these novel and difficult issues in a short period of time and with no clarity about the requirements for a class action beyond those in the Law Commission's report. In addition, he had not heard the full argument and reference to international authority presented to the Supreme Court of Appeal by able counsel.

Had the learned acting judge had the benefit of these arguments, and the parameters that had now been laid down for these types of applications, he would not have disposed of the application in such a summary way. Instead, he should have provided the appellants with an opportunity to correct and amplify their application in particulars of claim and further affidavits. He should then have given the respondents a chance to respond, and the appellants to reply, upon which the application could have been dealt with in the light of a full appreciation of the respective parties' cases.

'As that is the approach that should have been adopted,' Judge Wallis declared, 'the appeal must succeed, and the matter must be referred back to the High Court to be dealt with in accordance with the requirements of this judgment.'

In view of the fact that this was novel litigation, in which parties were largely operating in the dark, and the appellants might not gain much from the outcome in the long run, he ruled that all the parties should bear their own costs in respect of the appeal.

The bread distributors were not so fortunate. This time, the judgment was delivered by Judge of Appeal Robert Nugent, with the other four concurring. The justification for class actions, Judge Nugent noted, was that without this procedural device, claimants would be denied access to the courts. However, if 100 bread distributors could embark on an opt-in class action, there was no reason why they should not do so in their own names and take joint legal action, to which they were entitled.

The only argument advanced for proceeding by way of a class action instead of a joint action was that this would immunise the distributors against personal liability for costs. This did not seem to be a good reason for allowing a class action. On the contrary, personal liability for costs would help to restrain frivolous actions brought to force defendants into financial settlements, which was one of the dangers to be avoided in certifying class actions.

Although he would not close the door to 'opt-in' class actions, Judge Nugent stated, the circumstances would need to be exceptional, and nothing exceptional had been shown in this case. On these grounds, the claim to certification had to fail, and the appeal was dismissed. In view of the novelty of the claim, and its close association with the consumers' case, he also ruled that all the parties should pay their own costs.

The bread distributors now found themselves in a strange situation. The costs award against them in the Western Cape High Court was still hanging over their heads, but the Appeal Court decision in the bread consumer case meant that there was a general class action available to them if they could satisfy the criteria for the certification of a class. The millstone of trying to shoe-horn their cause of action into an infringement of the Bill of Rights had been removed by the way in which the law had been developed in the course of the consumer case. The Appeal Court's decision not to give the distributors the benefit of this widening of the net of possible class actions was perplexing, as was its reliance upon the novel concept of 'exceptional circumstances' to justify an 'opt-in' class action by bread distributors.

The case was ripe for ventilation in the highest court in the land. In order to get a hearing in the Constitutional Court, it is necessary to persuade it to grant leave to appeal. The necessary application was prepared, and was vigorously opposed by all the bread producers.

In the event, the Constitutional Court granted the bread distributors leave to appeal. The Chief Justice was absent, and the court was presided over by the Deputy Chief Justice, Dikgang Moseneke. A friend of the court, the Legal Resources Centre, joined the fray to sing the praises of a general class action, and a lot of probing questions were asked, as is usually the case.

In the course of preparing the appeal, the distributors' legal team enlisted the assistance of a recently retired professor of law at the University of Cape Town, Wouter de Vos. His input proved to be invaluable, and his appearance as junior counsel in the Constitutional Court was an enriching experience for a lawyer who had spent most of his career in the halls of academia rather than in the courts. Shortly after the hearing, Wouter was offered a position at a university in Perth, Australia, which he accepted.

The judgments in the Constitutional Court make for interesting reading. As previously, the helpful staff at the court itself made these more accessible to the general public by issuing an accompanying media release, summarised as follows:

In 2006, following complaints by bread distributors, the Competition Commission launched an investigation into the conduct of the respondents – the bread producers Pioneer, Tiger and Premier – and found them guilty of engaging in anti-competitive conduct.

In November 2012, Imraahn Mukaddam and other bread distributors applied to the Western Cape High Court for permission to bring a class action against the respondents. The application was refused. The Supreme Court of Appeal rejected an appeal on the grounds that the claims were bad in law, and that the distributors had failed to establish the 'exceptional circumstances' needed to institute a class action.

Now, in a majority judgment written by Justice Jafta, the Constitutional Court had overturned the judgments of the High Court and the Supreme Court of Appeal, holding that the High Court applied the incorrect test to Mukaddam's application. The correct standard, the Court had found, was to determine whether the institution of a class action would be in the interests of justice.

Acting Justice Mhlantla concurred with Justice Jafta save for parts of the judgment that circumscribed the reach of certification in class actions involving Bill of Rights claims. In her view, given the rationale for certification and the nature of class actions, the benefits of the certification process applied in all class action suits.

In a separate concurring judgment, Justice Froneman, with Justice Skweyiya concurring, noted that the development of the common law to provide for class actions in non-constitutional matters, undertaken by the Supreme Court of Appeal in the Children's Resources Centre Trust case, was a valuable contribution to the law, which provided flexible guidelines to apply to applications for the certification of class actions on a case-by-case basis.

However, in his view, the Supreme Court of Appeal's application of these guidelines to the applicant's potential claim in the proposed class action was too strict. He held further that it would be premature to finally determine, at this early stage of certification, that the applicant had no tenable claim in South African law.

Mukaddam had reason to celebrate. The Constitutional Court had set aside the costs award against him in the distributors' case, and he was given a fresh opportunity to advance the class action for bread distributors in the light of the change in the law that had been effected by the Supreme Court of Appeal in the consumer case, and the more generous approach of the Constitutional Court to his claims.

When the work started on quantifying the bread distributors' claims, it was found that the cartel had been so quickly and efficiently shut down that the claims were not as huge as initially thought. Two of the bread producers were willing to settle the class action rather than fight it out further.

Confidential negotiations followed between the attorneys for all the parties, bar Premier Foods, which as whistle-blower regarded itself as exempt from civil liability of the kind in question. The negotiations were successfully concluded without further litigation.

In November 2015, the Supreme Court of Appeal upheld Premier's stance. At the time of writing, it was unclear whether a further appeal to the Constitutional Court would follow. The bread distributors were not involved in that litigation, which was pursued by the consumers.

Playing a role in the creation of general class action in South African law has been one of the most significant achievements of Accountability Now. There is rich irony in the fact that a determined client drove us into the litigation after we had advised him that he would be ill-advised to take his case further. Imraahn Mukaddam's role in seeking justice for the distributors and consumers of bread has been recorded for posterity in the moving documentary film with the fitting title *Crumbs*. The internet blurb for the documentary says it all.

> *Crumbs* is the David versus Goliath story of Imraahn Mukaddam, the bread reseller who blew the whistle on bread price-fixing in South Africa. This documentary explores the turmoil Imraahn faces in taking on the corporate food machine in the quest for social justice. In 2007, the three largest bread manufacturers in South Africa formed one of the worst cartels in our country's history. Bread prices spiked, leaving less food on the table for the poorest of the poor. Slapped with a multi-billion-rand fine, the cartel was broken up, all because of the actions of one whistleblower: Imraahn Mukaddam. *Crumbs* is a tale of David versus Goliath – the front line in the moral struggle between greed versus humanism. The documentary explores the legal, financial and personal turmoil of Imraahn's fight against the corporate food machine in the quest for accountability and social justice.

The bread cartel case led to Mukaddam reinventing himself in numerous ways. He became involved in community television, and started playing a broader role as community activist.

Chapter 12

Dealing with National Commissioners of Police

———•———

'It's not what you have, it's how you use it.'
– Sipho 'Hotstix' Mabuse

THE GOVERNING alliance in the new South Africa, led by the ANC, follows a policy known as 'cadre deployment'. Officially entitled the 'Cadre Policy and Deployment Strategy', its stated purpose is to allow the ANC to gain control over 'key centres of power' as a means of advancing the 'national democratic revolution'.

What this means in practice is that it appoints party loyalists to positions of power and authority. This practice is not restricted to political appointments or positions in the civil service alone; according to careful research by Anthea Jeffery of the SAIRR, cadre deployment is also meant to extend ANC control over parastatals, the judiciary, the media, business, universities, and influential organisations in civil society. Needless to say, given these priorities, the issue of whether those people are actually qualified to fill those positions in conventional terms takes a back seat.

Cadre deployment is unconstitutional, and therefore actually illegal, but continues nevertheless. The SAPS is not exempted from this policy, despite the fact that policing is a profession, and dropping in cadres through the ceiling of such a complex organisation invariably has unintended consequences.

The first cadre to lead the police was Jackie Selebi, a former exile with strong struggle credentials. He was close to President Thabo Mbeki, who tried to shield him from prosecution on charges of corruption in the run-up to the ANC's fateful national conference at Polokwane in December 2007, where the 'Zuma tsunami' swept Mbeki and his cohorts out of power.

In his efforts to shield Selebi, Mbeki suspended the then national director of public prosecutions, Vusi Pikoli. Years later, Mbeki invoked 'national security' as an excuse for doing so, stating that he feared a confrontational backlash from police loyal to Selebi, which could have led to violence or 'even civil war'. These fears were not based in reality (no civil war erupted when Selebi was arrested), and certainly did not warrant the interference in Pikoli's independence or tenure, which is constitutionally guaranteed.

Selebi was eventually prosecuted, convicted, and sentenced to 15 years imprisonment, but was given medical parole due to a serious kidney complaint, and died shortly afterwards. Despite his cadre status and connectedness, the law was able to take its proper course, and the prosecution was able to discharge the heavy onus of proving him guilty of a corrupt relationship with Glen Agliotti, a Johannesburg businessman of the less than conventional kind.

The person chosen by newly appointed President Jacob Zuma to replace Selebi was a flamboyant KwaZulu-Natal politician, Bheki Cele, whom some journalists referred to as 'the cat in the hat', due to his fondness for wearing a variety of these head-warming items of clothing. There was no need to enquire into his pedigree in the ANC. Cele had served as MEC for community safety in President Jacob Zuma's province, KwaZulu-Natal, and was a well-known and popular ANC leader. Vitally, he had known President Zuma for more than 20 years.

The decision to 'deploy' him as national commissioner of police was clearly a political one that was not informed in any way by his knowledge or experience of police management. The high rates of crime, and the need to address the SAPS's apparent inability to prevent and combat crime, suggested that a 'big gun' should be appointed. Instead of selecting a professional policeman or woman, Zuma used his powers of appointment to push Cele into a position for which he was not suited.

Cele's bellicose attitude, his militarisation of the police, and his penchant for a 'shoot-to-kill' response to serious armed criminality endeared him to the public, reduced crime statistics, and deviated markedly from the human rights-oriented approach of the SAPS in the early years of democracy. The SAPS once again became a police force (rather than a police service), and the rate at which police were killed in the line of duty crept up alarmingly.

However, on 1 August 2010, it emerged that Cele had been busy in other ways as well. In a page one lead, the *Sunday Times* reported that Cele had concluded a 'dodgy' R500-million property deal with billionaire businessman Roux Shabangu that would result in the police moving their Pretoria headquarters to a building Shabangu had bought only the previous week. The building was aptly named 'Middestad'.

Cele had allegedly signed the deal to move SAPS top brass – including the minister of police Nathi Mthethwa, his deputy, Fikile Mbalula, and administrative staff – to Shabangu's building almost two months before he had bought it.

The deal had not at any stage gone out to tender, violating Treasury regulations that all contracts over R500 000 had to go through a competitive bid process. After three days of queries from the *Sunday Times*, the Department of Public Works could not explain why it had flouted Treasury rules.

Shabangu confirmed that he had bought the 18-storey Middestad Sanlam centre in Pretoria for R220-million the previous week, and claimed he was still 'negotiating' with the police. But the *Sunday Times* said it was in possession of a lease agreement for Middestad between Shabangu's company, Roux Property Fund, and the SAPS, signed by Cele and public works official M B Tlolane on 1 June. The lease would run for 10 years, and specified that cheques should be made out to Shabangu's company. Projected expenditure totalled more than R520 million.

SAPS headquarters was housed in the Wachthuis building just around the corner. It was owned by Encha Properties, which declined to disclose the rental it charged. However, a police insider said the Wachthuis lease was also worth about R500-million, and was set to run for another 10 years. Therefore, unless the Wachthuis lease was cancelled, taxpayers could be forking out almost R1-billion in the next decade to house SAPS headquarters.

According to the *Sunday Times*, senior officials had serious reservations about the move. 'They don't understand why you should rent a new building when there is enough space (at

Wachthuis),' it quoted an official close to police management as saying. For R500-million, the *Sunday Times* noted, at least 10 000 new constables could be patrolling South Africa's streets.

It also noted that Wachthuis owners, Encha Properties, belonged to the Moseneke family, who were close allies of former president Thabo Mbeki. Shabangu, on the other hand, appeared to be well connected with the Zuma government.

SAPS officials told the *Sunday Times* that Cele had also signed a deal to move police in Durban to another building Shabangu was negotiating to buy. Shabangu was in Durban that Friday, trying to clinch the deal, which he refused to elaborate on, saying negotiations were at a sensitive stage'.

He confirmed that police were due to move into his Pretoria building, claiming they wanted to leave Wachthuis as it was in poor condition. He also claimed the validity of Encha's Wachthuis lease was questionable. But Encha Properties CEO Dr Sedise Moseneke told the *Sunday Times* his company had a 'lawful lease' to accommodate police headquarters at Wachthuis, and denied that there was anything wrong with the building. Subsequent media reports quoted property sources as saying that the rental deal was three times higher than the going rate for office space in the same area.

This report set the alarm bells ringing at Accountability Now. The appropriate response, given that the *Sunday Times* protected it sources, was to complain to the Public Protector, Thuli Madonsela, about what appeared to be maladministration on a grand scale involving top SAPS brass.

It was not necessary to wait until Monday morning; the Office of the Public Protector has a dedicated email address for lodging complaints. So we sent off an email, asking the Public Protector to investigate the allegations contained in the *Sunday Times* report on the grounds that they seemed to reflect gross maladministration.

The Public Protector did so, and sent a preliminary report to Accountability Now for comment on the findings. This gave us an opportunity to draw attention to the requirements for the proper procurement of public goods and services, as set out in the Constitution and the Public Finance Management Act. In short, procurement is meant to conform to five criteria: equity, fairness, transparency, competitiveness, and cost-effectiveness. Cele was also given the chance to comment on the preliminary report. A final report followed, which recommended that a board of inquiry be appointed into his fitness to hold office.

In her final report, the Public Protector found that the conduct of the accounting officers of the SAPS (i.e. Cele) and the Department of Public Works (DPW) in respect of the lease was improper and unlawful. Accountability for budgetary control and the procurement of goods and services within all government departments lay with the accounting officer, who at all material times were the National Commissioner of the SAPS and the director general of the DPW. The National Commissioner, as the accounting officer of the SAPS, had acted in breach of those duties and obligations incumbent upon him in terms of the constitution and the PFMA.

Section 217 of the constitution, read with the PFMA and the Treasury regulations, required accounting officers to ensure that goods and services were procured in a fair, equitable, transparent, competitive, and cost-effective manner. Section 237 provided that all constitutional obligations be performed diligently. All conduct inconsistent with the constitution was legally invalid.

The National Commissioner had withdrawn all delegations in respect of the procurement of goods and services over an amount of R500 000 with effect from 30 September 2009. He was therefore solely responsible to ensure that the procurement of the lease, for as far as the involvement of the SAPS was concerned, complied with these legal prescripts.

The lease agreements with the Roux Property Fund (RPF) had been signed by the DPW and not the national commissioner of the SAPS, as had been alleged. However, the National Commissioner had signed a memorandum authorising funding for the Sanlam Middestad building lease, as well as a final SAPS needs analysis referring to the exact extent of accommodation available in the Sanlam building.

Although the SAPS had not signed the lease agreement, its involvement in the procurement process was improper as it had proceeded beyond the demand management phase and had further failed to implement proper controls, as required by the PFMA and relevant procurement prescripts.

In the process, the SAPS had failed to comply with section 217 of the constitution, the relevant provisions of the PFMA, Treasury regulations, and supply chain management rules and policies. This amounted to improper conduct and maladministration.

The conduct of the accounting officer of the SAPS was also in breach of those duties and obligations. The provisions required an accounting officer to ensure that goods and services were procured in a fair, equitable, transparent, competitive and cost-effective manner. This conduct was also improper, unlawful, and amounted to maladministration.

On the evidence available, the report noted, it could not be found that the deviation from required tender procedures had been motivated by an improper relationship between the preferred service provider (RPF) and the SAPS. The report recommended that the Minister of Police, assisted by the National Treasury, should take urgent steps to ensure that appropriate action was taken against the National Commissioner and other SAPS officials involved. The SAPS should implement appropriate measures to prevent a recurrence of contraventions of the relevant procurement legislation and prescripts.

The 'appropriate action' envisaged by the Public Protector took the form of the Moloi Board of Inquiry into Cele's conduct as well as the leases in Pretoria and Durban. The board did not have powers of search and seizure, or the power to subpoena unwilling witnesses. Shabangu did not give evidence, but Cele did, condemning himself in the process.

The board recommended that Cele be dismissed and investigated for corruption. The dismissal followed, but a corruption investigation did not, as Cele took the findings of the Board on review, alleging bias and irrationality. The review was eventually postponed indefinitely without being resolved, Cele found his way onto the list of ANC candidates for parliament in 2014, and then into the cabinet of Jacob Zuma, who had dismissed him as commissioner of police. At the time of writing, he was deputy minister of Agriculture, Forestry and Fisheries – a fate very different to that of Mbeki's man, Jackie Selebi.

Cele was succeeded as commissioner of police by Riah Phiyega, a social worker by training, with later experience as a parastatal board member. After the Marikana tragedy, in which a police task force shot and killed 34 striking miners and wounded 78 more, the Farlam Commission of Inquiry recommended that her fitness for office be investigated.

In September 2015, Zuma established a board of inquiry, chaired by Judge Cornelis Claassen and assisted by advocates Bernard Khuzwayo and Anusha Rawjee, to investigate Phiyega's conduct and her fitness to hold office. He then suspended her summarily in October, pending the outcome of the inquiry. Following widely publicised hearings, the board completed its work in late May 2016, and was due to report in August.

It is a poor reflection of the wisdom of South Africa's political leadership that three successive commissioners of police should fall from grace as Selebi, Cele and Phiyega have done in so short a period of time. Phiyega had barely been appointed when the Marikana tragedy took place. The unwillingness of the presidency to appoint a career policeman or woman to head the SAPS is lamentable, and can only be explained by a strong desire to exercise tight political control over the successive incumbents, lest they perform their duties in ways that do not suit the national leadership. The police, like all other civil servants, are constitutionally obliged to observe high standards of professional ethics and to deliver services fairly, equitably and without bias. It is a measure of the fragility of the South African state that this does not occur.

Cele's 'rehabilitation' is remarkable. Phiyega's testimony in front of the Farlam commission was deplorable. An attempt was made to cover up police activity on the day of the Marikana shooting, and sustained after evidence leaders had uncovered the truth, or part of it. Phiyega's performance under cross-questioning did not inspire confidence in her probity and integrity. Selebi's fate speaks for itself.

These outcomes will continue to plague our public administration until proper human-resource management practices are applied across the board, and the ANC terminates its cadre deployment policy that has so bedevilled our national development. Whether the political will exists to do so, in the interests of strong institutions and good governance aligned to the UN's sustainable development goals, remains to be seen.

Accountability Now will continue to work towards a dispensation in which accountability is exacted from all those in positions of authority, whether in the private or the public sector, and responsiveness to the needs of ordinary people is promoted. Accountability does matter; it is fundamental to the rule of law, which, in turn, is fundamental to peace, progress and prosperity.

Chapter 13

Firepool or Waterloo?
Accountability Now and Nkandla

———•———

*'There is no shame in strategic retreat if it lets you
remain strong enough to go after the enemy later.'*
– Jane Lindskold

WHEN THE late Mandy Rossouw – then a journalist with the
Mail & Guardian – broke the Nkandla story in 2009, she started
a saga that was still incomplete by mid-2016, when this book
went to press. Initially, the story seemed one of the mismanage-
ment of public funds, but over time it morphed into the EFF's
war-cry of 'Pay back the money!' – a demand addressed, vocif-
erously and repeatedly, at President Jacob Zuma.

Nkandla is the country seat of the Zuma clan in northern
KwaZulu-Natal, and has been for many years, going back to
the Anglo-Zulu wars of the 19th century. The land is owned by
a trust controlled by the Zulu king. Before Zuma rose to power,
it consisted of an unprepossessing cluster of rondavels. The
law allows for security enhancements to the property of presidents at the expense of the taxpayer. This chance was seized,
and a massive programme of works turned the homestead into
a badly built palace with many new features that had nothing
to do with the security of the president in residence, and much

more to do with an abuse of office, maladministration, and 'scope creep' in the course of the project, which was managed by the Department of Public Works. Among other things, the work was placed under the supervision of Zuma's private architect, who was subsequently sued for R155 million and, at the time of writing, was defending the civil case brought against him by the Special Investigating Unit (SIU), an entity that needs an instruction from the president to investigate any situation.

Once the media began to feed on the story of the excesses at Nkandla, it did not take long for a range of complaints to land on the desk of the Public Protector, Adv Thuli Madonsela. This prompted an investigation and led to the publication, in March 2014, of her celebrated report entitled *Secure in Comfort*. The report was then 'second-guessed' by parliament and the minister of police. In a comical interlude, the latter sought to protect his leader by characterising the swimming pool built during the renovations as a 'fire-pool', thus magically converting it into a security enhancement.

The governing alliance in parliament took the position that the remedial action required by the Public Protector was no more than a recommendation, and had no binding effect. How this could be argued, with a straight face, when the constitution itself says that 'The Public Protector has the power . . . to take appropriate remedial action' is one of the abiding mysteries of the entire saga. The president's legal representatives eventually abandoned this defence when the matter was finally argued in the Constitutional Court.

In December 2013, some months before the Public Protector released her report, a leaked copy was given copious coverage in the *Mail & Guardian*. This attracted the attention of Account-ability Now. On any proper analysis of the leaked report, things had run off the rails at Nkandla on a massive scale. The question was: what to do about it?

We decided that a criminal complaint would be the best way forward. This invokes the machinery of state, and puts the criminal justice administration into the loop. It can have a back-straightening effect on minor players in the malfeasance in question, leading to confessions, plea bargains, and deals for immunity from prosecution in exchange for a clean breast and useful information for catching the 'big fish'. Of course, with very big fish this does not necessarily happen rapidly, but it can happen, given time.

And so it came to pass that, at the crack of dawn on the day after the death of Nelson Mandela, I found myself in the charge office at the Cape Town Central Police Station with a letter of complaint in my hand. A Constable Ndebele was on duty, and was bored and tired at the end of his shift. Not much happened in the charge office at that hour.

He asked how he could help me, and when I indicated that I wanted to lay some charges, he ushered me toward a cubicle. He then produced the standard form for laying a complaint, and proceeded to fill it in. When we got to the part of the form where the offences had to be listed, I produced the letter of complaint, and suggested that he simply write 'see attached letter to the Western Cape Commissioner of Police'. He scanned the letter, and stiffened when he came to the name of the person against whom the complaint was being laid: 'Jacob G Zuma'.

'I think I should ask one of my superiors to help you,' he said.

'I don't think that's necessary,' I replied; 'this is just a formality, to put the ball into play.'

'No, I insist,' he responded, and scuttled off to the back office before I could argue the point further.

He was gone for a couple of minutes, and re-appeared looking crestfallen. Obviously reluctant to risk jeopardising their careers by accepting the complaint, his superiors had told him to get on with the job at hand.

The forms were duly filled in, I took the required oath, and left for the early service at St George's Cathedral, where the organist Barry Smith emerged from retirement to play a magnificent rendition of the National Anthem. This virtuoso performance was given to mark the passing of Madiba for a far larger congregation than usual, due to the news of Madiba's death and the presence of the Arch at the service. As a result, the Anglican Church was probably the first institution in South Africa, if not the world, to solemnly mark the passing of the great man.

A few months later, I received a call from Constable Ndebele. It emerged that he was facing disciplinary proceedings because he had accepted my complaint on behalf of Accountability Now. A quick interaction with police management put a stop to this misstep. Following the release of the Public Protector's final report on Nkandla in March 2014, the complaint was amplified by others filed by the DA and EFF. Strangely, the matter was not referred to the Hawks, which, given the nature of the charges, would have been the appropriate police unit to conduct the investigation. Instead, it was retained by Detective Services in Pretoria on the express instructions of the national commissioner of police, Riah Phiyega. This rankled with Hawks managers, but, given the command structures in the SAPS, there was little they could do to get their hands on the docket.

This situation changed when, in November 2014, the Constitutional Court gave its judgment in Glenister III. Emboldened by the additional powers afforded him under the new court-crafted dispensation, the head of the Hawks, General Anwa Dramat, reportedly called for the dockets about Nkandla to be transferred to his unit. This did not happen. Instead, the Minister of Police suspended Dramat on 23 December 2014 on the grounds of kidnapping allegations dating back several years which had, until then, been entirely ignored. To make matters worse, in terms of the amended legislation, the minister no longer had the power to suspend Dramat; this could only be done with the permission of parliament. However, no such permission was sought or obtained.

When it became apparent, in the course of civil litigation launched by the HSF assailing the suspension, that the minister had erred, further pressure was brought to bear on the hapless Dramat. He succumbed by resigning, and accepting a rather generous package. In March 2016, he was charged with the kidnapping. At the time of writing, this criminal case was still pending. Needless to say, nothing had come of the criminal charges laid by the three institutions mentioned earlier in respect of Nkandla, all of which based their complaints on the report of the Public Protector.

In place of an independent and effective criminal investigation into the excesses of Nkandla, which was clearly not on the cards, the opposition parties in parliament turned to the civil courts to review the strange gyrations of the cabinet and the ANC majority in parliament, all aimed at whitewashing the malfeasance apparent from the report of the Public Protector.

First the DA launched review proceedings in the High Court with the overarching aim of establishing the extent of the powers of the Public Protector. This went hand in hand with its court action in respect of the chief operating officer of the SABC, Hlaudi Motsoeneng. This worthy had similarly treated adverse findings by the Public Protector about his conduct at the SABC as a recommendation, which he was at liberty to ignore.

In February 2014, in a report entitled *When Governance and Ethics Fail*, the Public Protector found that Motsoeneng – then still acting COO – had been 'dishonest' and had been allowed to operate above the law. It recommended that the SABC board take corrective action against him for lying about his matric certificate, raising his salary from R1,5 million to R2,4 million, and irregularly increasing the salaries of other staff members. Despite the report, Motsoening was permanently appointed to his position in July 2014.

In 2015, the DA launched a court application to try to force the SABC to implement Madonsela's report and to set aside Motsoeneng's appointment. The court ruled that Madonsela's report was legally binding, and ordered the SABC to stage a disciplinary hearing. The hearing was held in December, but cleared Motsoeneng of any wrongdoing. At the time of writing, he was still – visibly – in place, but fighting a rearguard action in the form of appeals against findings by Judge Dennis Davis of the Western Cape High Court that his full appointment was irrational, and that neither he nor the SABC would be given leave to appeal.

But back to Nkandla: the EFF then took the bull by the horns and made a direct approach to the Constitutional Court, alleging that it would be in the interests of justice to reach a swift conclusion in respect of the various issues that its demand to 'Pay back the money' had raised. When the Constitutional Court indicated that it was prepared to give the EFF a hearing on the matter, the DA swiftly changed its focus and also approached the Constitutional Court. The Public Protector herself joined in the proceeding to protect her turf and her entitlement to take appropriate remedial action. The stage was set for a mighty confrontation.

To the surprise of many long-standing observers of the 'scorched earth' strategy usually adopted by those advising President Zuma, the confrontation did not materialise. In the weeks prior to the hearing, Zuma's team put out feelers about settling the matter, and even made an open tender to dispose of it without a fight. The tender was not accepted, and argument was heard. Zuma then threw in the towel, mirroring his eventual response to the arms deals litigation. All that remained was for the court to spell out the law, and what needed to be done to 'pay back the money'.

The judgment was not long in coming. The Chief Justice himself delivered it in full, live on television, on 31 March. When he read Order 5 of the judgment, he placed particular emphasis on the word 'only' in the sentence reading:

> 5. The National Treasury must determine the reasonable costs of those measures implemented by the Depart-

ment of Public Works at the President's Nkandla homestead that do not relate to security, namely the visitors' centre, the amphitheatre, the cattle kraal, the chicken run and the swimming pool only.

6. The National Treasury must determine a reasonable percentage of the costs of those measures which ought to be paid personally by the President.

The emphasis on the word 'only' set the alarm bells ringing at Accountability Now. This is because the report of the Public Protector made it crystal clear that *all* non-security enhancements to Nkandla paid for by the taxpayer via the DPW were for the president's account, and only truly security-related enhancements for that of the taxpayer. Specifically, the report said the president should:

> Take steps, with the assistance of the National Treasury and the SAPS, to determine the reasonable cost of the measures implemented by the DPW at his private residence that do not relate to security, and which include the Visitors' Centre, the amphitheatre, the cattle kraal and chicken run, the swimming pool . . . [and] . . . Pay a reasonable percentage of the cost of the measures as determined with the assistance of National Treasury, also considering the DPW apportionment document.

As fate would have it, Accountability Now met Adv Madonsela and her Cape Town Office chief, Adv Sune Griessel, on 1 April 2014, the day after the judgment. Although Nkandla was not on the agenda, there was much to celebrate in respect of the court's findings, especially as regards the binding and enforceable nature of the 'appropriate remedial action' the Public Protector may require after investigating a complaint. It would no longer be possible to push her reports aside. Anyone who was aggrieved by prescribed remedial action would have to take this on judicial review. If this was not feasible, the unhappy respondent would be left with no alternative but to take the remedial steps required. In the case of Nkandla, this would involve complying with the passage in the *Secure in Comfort* report quoted above. However, the Nkandla matter did not follow a course which anyone could properly describe as 'usual'.

The highest court in the land had been asked to apply itself to the matter, and to give its guidance. While the focus of attention was always on the extent of the powers of the Public Protector, the court did express itself on the quantum of the payment to be made in orders 5 and 6. This had the effect of considerably reducing the sum of money to be paid back, and of diluting the nature of the remedial action required by the Public Protector.

We raised this concern during our meeting with Adv Madonsela. Guy Lloyd-Roberts, a director of Accountability Now, and the late Professor Tim Dunne, then our chair of trustees, expressed concern that the effectiveness of her office would be undermined if the error in the judgment was not addressed.

Adv Madonsela expressed her sympathy for our position, and invited us to lodge a complaint. Later that same day, the president took to national television to apologise to the nation, and the ANC secretary general, Gwede Mantashe, held a media conference during which he issued a significant invitation to the South African public. Accountability Now decided to accept the invitation, and wrote Comrade Secretary General a letter. Some extracts follow:

4 April 2016

Dear Secretary General

Re: Our response to your press conference 1st April 2016

1. During your press conference on the evening of 1 April 2016, you appealed to the public to engage with the ANC regarding the implications of the Constitutional Court judgment concerning the non-security enhancements to the President's private home at Nkandla and more generally, as we understood you, regarding the trajectory of our hard-won constitutional democracy under the rule of law in which openness, accountability and responsiveness are all foundational values in the order of the day. We welcome your invitation, and have decided to act on it.

2. You may recall that we have engaged with you previously regarding the suitability of the President for the high office he holds . . .

3. In June last year, we wrote to you again to suggest the recall of the President by the ANC due to his involvement in the corrupt settlement package accepted by Mxolisi Nxasana in exchange for his resignation as National Director of Public Prosecutions and also because the President illegally, and in a manner that amounts to defeating the ends of justice, gave an undertaking to the President of Sudan that he would not be arrested in South Africa. President Robert Mugabe, then head of the AU, made our President's undertaking public before both the Full Bench of the High Court in Pretoria and the Supreme Court of Appeal confirmed the illegality of not arresting al-Bashir. Should the matter

actually reach a hearing in the Constitutional Court it is likely to rule the same way, thereby bringing the fitness for office of the President into question once more . . .

4. As regards the Nxasana debacle, . . . we have laid criminal charges against the President and the Minister of Justice. The docket is under investigation by the Hawks. There are also civil proceedings pending in relation to the matter, which, if successful, will throw further light on the illegality involved in paying out Nxasana the undiscounted balance of his ten-year term of office in order to get rid of him, allegedly because of his willingness to prosecute corruption in high places. The outcome of the civil proceedings will inform the further conduct of the criminal case.

5. In your capacity as Secretary General of the ANC, you are doubtless aware and advised that:

    - the Al-Bashir case is unlikely to end well for the President;
    - the Commission of Inquiry into the fitness for office of his appointee, Riah Phiyega, our current National Commissioner of Police, is unlikely to give her a clean bill of health;
    - the review of the withdrawal of 783 corruption charges against the President himself, whether or not it is won in the courts, reflects poorly on the choice of leader of the ANC especially as his former financial adviser, Schabir Shaik, was sentenced to 15 years imprisonment for corrupting the President;
    - the prospects of the applicants' success in the litigation challenging the removal from office of Nxasana are good, which will lead to his reinstatement as NDPP;
    - the legal challenge to the cabinet-endorsed choice of Berning Ntlemeza as head of the Hawks has merit;

- the underlying reasons for the friction between the Minister of Finance and the Hawks will, if made public in greater detail, plunge the President into yet another crisis involving his integrity, probity, and fitness for office;
- the name of the Zuma family is implicated in the 'Panama Papers' corruption data leak from the legal firm Mossack Fonseca in Panama, lending credence to the denied claims by Julius Malema that the President recently took a vast amount of cash to Dubai for the Gupta family;
- the ongoing harassment of the Public Protector by the Hawks is both counterproductive and ill-considered;
- the decision of the ANC majority in the National Assembly to decline the well-reasoned request of the Public Protector for additional funding is lamentable, and ought to be reversed forthwith so as to ensure the dignity and effectiveness of that office, as is constitutionally required;
- none of the foregoing factors does anything positive to grow the national economy, and all of them hasten the looming financial downgrades of South Africa to junk status;
- due to the negative implications of junk status for the economy, the ability of the state to respect, protect, promote and fulfil the rights in the Bill of Rights, particularly the expensive pro-poor socio-economic rights, is placed in jeopardy;
- Nene-gate and the irregular nuclear build programme as well as allegations of state capture and the inability of the President to make sound appointments due to his compromised and conflicted status contribute to the negative outlook for the economy;

- The effect on the political popularity of the ANC in a climate in which social security services are cut back; the public administration is shrunk; and housing, health care and education are not delivered on the scale to which the public have become accustomed will be negative.

6. We are obviously not privy to the confidential deliberations of the National Executive Committee of the ANC on which you serve. We would hope that the facts and factors listed above are all given due weight in its deliberations, and that it has due regard to the confidential market research on voting trends which the ANC conducts.

7. We respectfully submit that there is much to commend the immediate recall of the President, and we ask that the views of branches be democratically canvassed so that the NEC, as the highest decision-making body of the ANC between conferences, can be put into a position to give well-informed reconsideration to its decision not to recall the President at this delicate time in a dangerous year.

8. In our list of bullet points set out above, we have tried to concentrate on the future as much as possible. Like all patriotic South Africans, we are concerned that the international, and indeed local, perception of the sustainability, viability and probity of the country as an investment destination is adversely affected by all of the facts and factors we have listed for you. As the Minister of Finance has pointed out, it is essential to stimulate economic growth of the kind that creates jobs in large numbers for the currently unemployed youth of the country. This will not happen if the country is downgraded to junk status, and junk status is more probable

under the leadership of the President than if he is replaced as leader. The reverse he has suffered in the trenchantly worded decision on Nkandla by the Constitutional Court has served to strengthen the rand, as speculators seek to profit from his potential political demise. There is much for the ANC to cogitate upon in this development.

9.   . . . The debacle over the non-security enhancements to Nkandla has unfortunately not ended with the judgment of the Constitutional Court. In his apology to the nation on 1 April 2016, the President let it be known that it was always his intention to comply with the remedial action of the Public Protector as set out in her *Secure in Comfort* report . . . According to clause 11.1 of that report, the President must 'Take steps, with the assistance of the National Treasury and the SAPS, to determine the reasonable cost of the measures implemented by the DPW at his private residence that do not relate to security, and which include the Visitors' Centre, the amphitheatre, the cattle kraal and chicken run, [and] the swimming pool . . . '

10.   It is plain . . . that it was the intention of the Public Protector that all of the measures that do not relate to security that were implemented and paid for by the DPW are covered . . . The five items listed are obviously set out as examples of the kind of measures that do not relate to security, and they are not an exhaustive list on any proper interpretation of the words used by the Public Protector . . .

11.   If regard is had to the report itself as an aid to interpretation, then it is plain that many more items than the five examples listed are at play in the investigation, including but not limited to air-conditioning, the sewerage upgrade, paving, and professional fees of various

kinds that arose because of what the Public Protector rightly calls 'scope creep' in the project of the DPW at Nkandla. Indications are that these additional items and features could have cost in excess of R40 million.

12. While the Constitutional Court has very properly and correctly described the remedial action quoted above as binding and enforceable, its orders relating to the remedial action required of the President by the Public Protector are in effect a dilution, probably to a value measured in millions of rands, of the Public Protector's requirements . . .

13. The error in the orders 5 and 6 which gives rise to the ambiguity described above is best cleared up by the President himself announcing publicly that he understands orders 5 and 6 to mean that he must pay the full reasonable costs of the five items listed in order 5, and a reasonable percentage of such other measures as do not relate to security as determined by Treasury in order 6 . . .

14. As regards the impeachment debate in the National Assembly tomorrow, we would urge the ANC to allow its members a free and secret ballot in that debate so as to enable them to exercise unfettered oversight over the head of the executive as is their constitutional obligation, and also to facilitate the exacting of accountability on the part of the President . . .

15. We are willing to engage with you further should you so desire. We respectfully ask that you acknowledge receipt of this letter and let us have your substantive reply both on the possibility of recalling the President and on the enforcement of the Nkandla case order of court as soon as is possible.

At the same time, we wrote to the Public Protector to record our concerns about the dilution of the thrust of the remedial action. This is what we said:

4 April 2016

Dear Adv Madonsela

Re: The possible irregular dilution of the remedial action ordered by you in your 'Secure in Comfort' report on Nkandla in the wording of Orders 5 and 6 of the unanimous Constitutional Court judgment in the matter handed down on 31 March 2016

1. We are concerned, as we explained at our meeting in Cape Town on 1 April 2016, that the wording of the court order in the Nkandla matter may be interpreted in such a way as to dilute, erroneously and irregularly so, the effect of the remedial action you require of the President in relation to measures implemented at Nkandla by the Department of Public Works at taxpayers' expense which do not relate to security.

2. We respectfully refer you to para [10] of the judgment where the relevant part of your report is quoted with approval and without qualification by the Court. We ask you to compare clauses 11.1.1 and 11.1.2 of your report with the provisions of orders 5 and 6 of the order handed down on 31 March 2016.

3. In its discussion of the remedial action required in all the circumstances, the Court does not disclose any basis for diluting your report by unilaterally changing your wording 'and which include' as a reference to five examples of measures which do not relate to security to 'namely . . . only', which suggest, in order 5, a closed and exclusive list of measures that do not relate to security.

4. This suggestion is compounded by the use of the words 'those measures' in the two orders in a manner that ambiguously seems to indicate that 'those measures' are confined only to the five examples of the most egregious measures unrelated to security that you mentioned as examples in your report's clause 11.1.1.

5. Your report itself makes it abundantly clear that the five examples you cite are but the tip of the iceberg of expenditure incurred that does not relate to security. In this regard the various professional fees, the air-conditioning supplied, the upgrade to the sewerage system at Nkandla, and the extensive paving, estimated to have cost in excess of R 40 million, are but a few expensive instances in which all or part of the expenditure incurred is not related to security.

6. If the President and the National Treasury are going to interpret orders 5 and 6 of the judgment as being limited in a way not foreshadowed either in your report or in the body of the judgment itself, it is going to be necessary to approach the court to clarify and, if necessary, amend its order so that proper effect is given to the binding and enforceable nature of the remedial action you have specified.

7. We attach a letter to the Secretary General of the ANC in which we raise, inter alia, the matter of the interpretation of the court order.

8. Obviously, if the President is advised to heed our plea and lets it be known that he accepts that the court order does not irregularly dilute your remedial action, then no harm will have been done.

9. Conversely, if the President seeks to narrowly construe the orders so as to limit his personal liability to the five items mentioned in order 5, then it will be necessary

for you to defend the integrity, dignity and effectiveness of your office again.

10. It is not for us to say how you should go about doing so; there are various methods and strategies available including negotiation, mediation and further litigation to clarify the position.

11. For now, please regard this letter as an official letter of complaint that the wording of orders 5 and 6 has, or may have, irregularly diluted the ambit and effect of your remedial actions as specified in clauses 11.1.1 and 11.1.2 of your *Secure in Comfort* report.

12. We would respectfully suggest that you take the matter of our complaint up with the Treasury and, of course, with the President. If both show respect for the true ambit of your report, and construe the provisions of orders 5 and 6 in a way that does not limit the work required of Treasury to the five items set out in order 5, our complaint will be satisfied.

13. If, however, either of them interprets the orders to mean that the President is somehow magically absolved from repaying a reasonable percentage of all the other measures implemented at Nkandla, over and above the five items set out in order 5, then it will be necessary for you, and possibly the applicants in both matters, to apply to court to correct the erroneous interpretation of the order upon which the President and/or the Treasury may seek to rely. As we have pointed out to the ANC, the matter is urgent in that tight time limits have been set by the court.

We went to considerable trouble to ensure that Mantashe received his letter. This was confirmed well before the impeachment debate, itself a controversial procedure with no real precedent.

Some argued that an inquiry should precede the debate, and that the president should be obliged to appear before a committee of parliament to justify his actions and explain his decisions in respect of Nkandla and the adverse findings made against him not only by the Public Protector but also by the highest court in the land.

In the event, the ANC used its majority in the National Assembly to defeat the impeachment motion brought by the DA. We remained concerned that orders 5 and 6 of the Nkandla judgment required adjustment. This could be done by a court of its own volition. We made noises in the media and on television about the mistake or 'patent error' in the judgment, all to no avail. The Constitutional Court was not going to correct its own motion. Here is a single example of the trouble we took to draw public attention to the snafu in the judgment, in the form of an article published in *Business Day* in April 2016:

> *Final judgment on Nkandla may be Waterloo for Zuma*
> Much muddy water has flowed under the bridge since March 2014, when the 'Secure in Comfort' final report of the Public Protector about security enhancements at the Nkandla homestead occupied by the President and some members of his family was made public. On 9 February 2016, the Constitutional Court heard two applications for direct access to it concerning whether the failure to comply with the remedial action set out in that report constituted a breach of constitutional duties by the National Assembly and the President himself. The applications were brought by the Economic Freedom Fighters and the Democratic Alliance. Corruption Watch was given leave to be admitted as a friend of the court. The Public Protector

took part in the applications in order to defend her powers and argue on their ambit.

The investigation of the security enhancements by the Public Protector revealed that a cattle kraal, chicken run, swimming pool, visitors centre and amphitheatre, among other things, were built at state expense as part of the public works project at Nkandla. Her report concluded that state funds should not have been used for non-security enhancements to the homestead, and her remedial action was that the president must, with the assistance of the police and the minister of finance, determine the reasonable costs of those features and repay to the state a reasonable proportion of the expenses incurred at Nkandla in the course of the project.

The president and the National Assembly, in the purported exercise of its duty to hold the executive to account, took steps which they contended amount to compliance with the remedial action required by the Public Protector. The Minister of Police produced a report in May 2015 in which he found that no funds were payable by the President for the non-security enhancements. To get to this conclusion required some convoluted reasoning, which, to the astonishment of some, the Minister continues to defend.

The EFF and DA complained that the measures taken fell short of compliance with the Public Protector's remedial action and that the Minister's report was irregularly obtained.

The Public Protector and both applicants sought clarity from the court on the nature and extent of the power to take remedial action that the Public Protector has in terms of section 182(1)(c) of the Constitution. They submitted that her remedial actions are binding and enforceable unless set aside by a court of law and cannot be diluted, ignored or circumvented by other organs of State which are constitutionally obliged to ensure the protection of her dignity and effectiveness.

Both the President and the Speaker initially took up the position that the decisions of the Public Protector are not binding on them but in argument this contention was not persisted in by the President's counsel.

The Minister of Police stoutly contended that his report was valid and lawful. He intended, so he argued, to complement rather than subvert the report of the Public Protector.

Corruption Watch complained that the failure properly to implement the remedial action required undermined ethical standards and impaired the struggle against procurement corruption in SA.

The declaratory order sought to the effect that the President has violated his oath of office by acting in breach of his constitutional obligations in the manner in which he has conducted himself in relation to the investigation and report by the Public Protector was resisted on the whimsical basis that we live in "delicate times and a dangerous year". This argument attempts to wish away the powers of the courts sitting in constitutional matters. They "must declare any . . . conduct that is inconsistent with the Constitution is invalid to the extent of its inconsistency."

Against this background, the actual findings of the Constitutional Court are instructive. In essence every contention by the respondents with which the applicants did not agree was unanimously rejected by all eleven judges sitting in the matter. The judgment is a magnificent and monumental re-affirmation of the true nature of our constitutional democracy. It magisterially traverses the foundational values at play, the scope of the work of Chapter

Nine institutions that support constitutional democracy and the duties of the President, both as head of state and the national executive. While all due deference to the doctrine of the separation of powers is given, the National Assembly does not emerge unscathed. Its gyrations aimed at protecting the President against liability for the non-security upgrades are described as inconsistent with the duty of parliament to hold the executive to account. Despite the "delicate time in a dangerous year" submission on behalf of the President, the declaratory order he sought to avoid was made, on the basis that the court is obliged to do so according to the explicit words of the Constitution. The possibility of a bona fide error on the part of the President, whether due to wrong legal advice or otherwise, is regarded by the Court as irrelevant. A breach of a constitutional duty remains a breach, whether or not it is occurs due to a bona fide error.

From the point of view of the Public Protector, the judgment buries for all time the contentions that her remedial action power, derived from the Constitution, is anything other than binding and enforceable, unless it is framed in terms that are not intended by her to be binding and enforceable. This is not the case in respect of the *Secure in Comfort* report of March 2014. In essence the stance adopted in the Supreme Court of Appeal in the matter between the DA and the SABC is followed, in terms that are far more trenchantly set out for the avoidance of any doubt as to the thrust of the judgment and its interpretation of the ambit of the power to take remedial action accorded to the Public Protector by the Constitution in order to protect the public.

The judgment is also a strong endorsement of the rule of law and the foundational value of accountability in the constitutional order in place. It deals firmly and sternly with the conduct of the President and the National Assembly which falls short of constitutional muster insofar as their respective responses to the report of the Public Protector are concerned. The Speaker of the National Assembly ought to hang her head in shame for allowing the matter to take the convoluted course which it followed in the National Assembly. Her attitude that the Constitution, our supreme law, is no more than a "set of guidelines" is evident; her lack of impartiality in presiding over the Nkandla issues so as to shield the President from accountability is lamentably plain and the odious political posturing of the majority in the National Assembly, all meekly accepting instructions from Luthuli House without regard to their constitutional duties, is exposed. The President, the Minister of Police and the National Assembly have received their come-uppance from the Court. Conduct that is inconsistent with the Constitution is invalid. Their conduct in relation to the Nkandla debacle has been shown, to the satisfaction of the Court, to be inconsistent with the Constitution.

The relief granted by the Court is wide-ranging. It is declaratory, mandatory and supervisory in nature. Unfortunately, instead of fully implementing the remedial action required it appears to limit the President's liability to only five items whereas the Public Protector's report is far more wide ranging. In the light of recent revelations regarding the scope of non-security work done, the relief granted may not be framed widely enough to cover the true indebtedness of the President in respect of all of the non-security enhancements at Nkandla. Covered walkways, air-conditioning, meranti doors and other items have come to light, in a report by a whistle-blower who ought to know, during the period after the case was heard.

It is to be hoped that this development and the possible error and ambiguity in the orders granted will not lead to further skirmishing and delays.

The judgment is a test of the commitment of the ANC to the rule of law and the sanctity of the values of our constitution. South Africa can ill afford a president who breaks the law at all, but especially so at a time when the economic ratings agencies are pondering a downgrade to junk status. Whether the ANC is prepared to act appropriately on these sad facts remains to be seen. Its initial reactions are an insult to the intelligence of the people of South Africa. The president's apology on 1 April was mechanical and insincere. Gwede Mantashe's press conference, in which the President did not participate, was aimed at putting spin on the outcome, while the Speaker's unrepentant attitude during her 3 April press conference was disgracefully lamentable. The interests of the country are not served by the puny attempts at damage control that the ANC has developed to date. Hopefully something more positive and appropriate will be forthcoming in time.

When we became deafened by the silence of the ANC and the Public Protector, neither of whom responded substantively to the correspondence referred to above, we decided to await the input of the National Treasury, and the response of the court.

In due course, and with a day to spare, the National Treasury presented the Constitutional Court with a calculation of the president's indebtedness which was clearly limited to the five items listed in order 5. It came to R7,8 million, a fraction of the amount the president truly owes on any sensible interpretation of the Public Protector's report.

With unseemly haste, the court accepted the Treasury report, and ordered the president to personally pay the calculated amount. It was apparent that the court would not attend to the error of its own motion. We pinned our hopes on the Public Protector, and wrote her the following email on 18 May:

> Dear Adv Madonsela
>
> It emerged in debate in the National Assembly yesterday that the President appears to be interpreting orders 5 and 6 in the Constitutional Court Nkandla matter in the manner foreshadowed in paragraph 13 of our letter to you of 4 April 2016.
>
> In the circumstances, we complain that your report and the remedial action set out in it have been unlawfully diluted due to the error in the judgment, and we respectfully request that you and the applicants join in requesting the correction of the patent error in the judgment by the court as a matter of urgency.

We received no response. We tried again on 30 June:

> Dear Adv Madonsela
>
> 1. On 4 April this year, Accountability Now gave you an official complaint that your report called *Secure in Comfort* had been illegally diluted by the narrow scope of the order granted in the Nkandla litigation by the Constitutional Court. While we appreciate that you have no power to investigate court decisions, what is at stake here is not an investigation in the usual sense but an order of court that has resulted in prejudice to the public purse which, as a party to the relevant litigation, you are well placed to address. No investiga-

tion is indicated, only the correction of a patent and expensive error in the order made by the Constitutional Court.

2. At the same time we furnished you with a copy of the letter of the same date which we wrote to the Secretary General of the ANC, paragraphs 9 *et seq.* of which are relevant to the content of this letter. Both letters are on our website for public consumption, due to the wide public interest in securing a just outcome in the Nkandla litigation.

3. Clearly, the President has not chosen to construe the order in a way that protects the dignity and effectiveness of your office, as is required by section 181(3) of the Constitution, despite our respectful invitation in the letter to the ANC Secretary General that he do so. The taxpayer is also out of pocket for a great deal of money due to the incorrect and unduly narrow ambit of the order granted.

4. It is apparent to us and to more thoughtful members of the media . . . that the applicants, the *amicus curiae*, and your legal team in the Concourt have won an order that considerably dilutes the remedial action actually required by you in your report.

5. There is much speculation as to how this could have happened. This is not helpful. What would be helpful would be the launching, preferably by you, of a short and simple application under Rule 42 of the Uniform Rules of Court. The Constitutional Court has the power, both *mero motu*, and on application of any party affected, to vary its order so as to correct the patent error in it to the extent that the error requires variation of the order.

6. It is clear from the Court's acceptance of the calculation presented to it earlier this week that it is not contem-

plating any *mero motu* variation of the order it made, probably due to the fact that the true ambit of your report, when compared with its order, has not been properly drawn to its attention. Whatever the reason, it is plain that it is not in the interests of justice that the order containing the patent error be allowed to stand.

7. Kindly advise us of the fate of our complaint mentioned above.

8. We are particularly interested to know whether you or any affected party (notably the applicants, the EFF and DA) are contemplating or preparing an application under Rule 42. Lest you are unable to deal with this query yourself, to the extent that it involves the other affected parties, we are copying this email to them and their counsel so that they may make their position known both to you and to us. Ideally all four affected parties should collaborate in seeking to vary the order and thereby correct the patent error in it. Anything less than the necessary correction would amount to the turning of a blind eye to an expensive miscarriage of justice, not as regards the merits of the judgment in question, on which the Court was excellent, but as regards the quantum of the reasonable costs of non-security related enhancements to the Nkandla homestead which it orders the president to pay. We respectfully point out that as the author of the "Secure in Comfort" report, you are the person best placed to elucidate its ambit, to the extent that any such elucidation may be required. As we construe your report, it is plain ex facie the report itself that there has been a dilution of the remedial action you required to be taken.

9. Please acknowledge receipt of this email.

Yours in accountability.

The Public Protector did not acknowledge receipt of the letter, or respond to a telephone message. It seemed that she had gone to ground.

Next, we sought to lobby the political parties. As James Selfe of the DA had been at school with one of our directors, Guy Lloyd-Roberts, it seemed that this was a good link to exploit in the search for accountability in relation to the content of the judgment. Disappointingly, Guy drew a blank from the DA. In later correspondence, dated 11 July 2016, Selfe explained the DA's position in the following terms:

> . . . [O]f course the point is a good one. I discussed the matter with our team at the time the judgment was handed down, and again subsequently once this matter started to gain some media traction.
>
> The Chief Justice was quite emphatic when he specified the items for which Zuma had to pay. Our team think that that was deliberate, and that he wanted finality on the matter. To reopen the matter would open up new and costly avenues of litigation and counter-litigation, relating to what was 'included' in the Public Protector's report. Frankly, at this point, we don't have the resources to pursue this.
>
> Besides, we tend to engage in litigation to establish legal principles. In this case it was to establish the binding nature of the remedial action ordered by the Public Protector. We started this strategy by seeking a court determination on the SABC report, since the remedial action in that report was far clearer and less ambiguous. As you know, we achieved the right outcome in the SCA and we were just turning our attention (in the Western Cape High Court) to the Nkandla report, using the SCA

ruling, when the EFF applied for direct access to the Con-court. The legal principle has now been firmly established by the apex court. We see little merit in pursuing the matter further. This is also the professional advice we have received from our legal team.

We are, at the same time, carefully considering what is meant by 'personally pay'. In our view it was clearly the Court's intention that Zuma, and not his allies or friends, should pay the money. You will also have noticed that we are going after him for the tax he ought to have paid. Some of these aspects may result in further litigation.

After digesting this email, Accountability Now decided to communicate with the last remaining party in the matter, the EFF. The chairman of the EFF, Dali Mpofu SC, is a senior advocate of the Johannesburg Bar, and enjoys a good collegial relationship with the lawyers of Accountability Now. After talking to him on the phone on 12 July, it was a pleasure for me to record the upshot in an email, which read in part:

Thank you for phoning me back and for the reassurance that the matter of a Rule 42 application in respect of the snafu in the CC Nkandla judgment will receive the attention of the EFF legal team after the municipal elections on 3 August. I am very relieved to hear this, as there are millions at stake, as well as the further opportunity to hold JZ to account properly for the excesses of Nkandla. 'Pay back the money redux', if you like.

One afterthought concerning the timing of the EFF intervention. You don't want a 'full and final settlement' concluded before the Rule 42 application is actually launched. It would accordingly be prudent for the attorneys of record of the EFF to write to the attorneys representing government and those representing JZ warning them of the need for correction of the patent error in the orders 5 and 6 in the judgment so as to show greater fidelity to the report of the Public Protector styled 'Secure in Comfort'. Admonish them not to attempt any novations, full and final settlements or other nefarious tricks.

Also, please note that there is a lot of unanswered correspondence at www.accountabilitynow.org.za concerning the error in the judgment both with the OPP and with the ANC; it could be used as grist to the mill in the application, especially as the error was drawn to the attention of both as early as 4 April 2016. Simply search using "Nkandla" in the internal search engine on the site. None of the correspondence has been replied to yet; if any replies do come in, which seems unlikely after so much time has elapsed, we will be sure to let you know."

At the time of writing, the country was in the grip of a municipal election campaign. The matter of holding the president to final account on Nkandla would have to await the calmer waters of the post-election period. At least Accountability Now could say that it had played its part in exacting accountability for the malfeasance and misfeasance at Nkandla.

Epilogue: The idea is right, its time is now

---

*'Service to others is the rent you pay for
your room here on earth.'*
– Muhammad Ali

LIKE THE work of housewives of yesteryear, the task of preventing and combating corruption is never done. This perennial problem is because of human nature. Research has revealed that in any given society, about 10 per cent of people are incorruptible, about 10 per cent will always behave corruptly; and about 80 per cent could go either way, depending on the circumstances. A lack of deterrents, poor understanding of the implications of acting corruptly, poor law enforcement, impunity from the consequences, and a culture of entitlement are all circumstances that stoke the incidence of corruption.

Conversely, strong institutions backed by strong laws that are efficiently implemented; an educated public savvy to the corrosive nature of corruption; independent and effective anti-corruption machinery; a functional criminal justice system with the resources and capacity to arrest, prosecute and convict those involved in corruption; and a culture of responsible, accountable and responsive governance both generally and in relation to the procurement of public goods and services all combine to create circumstances in which the corrupt cannot thrive.

In November 2015, Accountability Now partnered with the Konrad Adenauer Foundation to present a Pan African Conference on Combating Corruption. Held in Cape Town, the conference was attended by a variety of role players from the legal professions, the judiciary, and civil society, both in South Africa and other African countries. At the end of the proceedings, delegates adopted the following resolution:

Cape Town Declaration, 5 November 2015

1. **Noting** the corrosive and pervasive nature of corruption in the world today, both in the private and in the public sectors.
2. **Identifying** corruption as a symptom of moral depravity, inimical to respect for and promotion of human rights, especially those of the poor and marginalised.
3. **Recognising** that it is the duty of states, commercial enterprises and all right thinking people to prevent and combat corruption because corruption is generally a serious and deplorable crime.
4. **Appreciating** that constitutional democracy under the rule of law and social stability are not served when corruption is endemic.
5. **Noting** that the widely accepted criteria for effective and successful anti-corruption entities include specialization by, training of, independence for, guaranteed resources for and security of tenure of staff of anti-corruption entities.
6. **Acknowledging** that corruption in Africa has reached

levels that threaten and undermine economic progress and growth throughout the continent despite the adoption and domestication of international, continental and regional instruments of international law that commit most countries in Africa to prevent , combat, investigate and prosecute corruption.

7. **Concluding that** corruption with impunity is inhibiting investment, increasing the cost of conducting business, undermining service delivery and exacerbating poverty in Africa and that corruption must be curbed to facilitate higher and more equitable economic growth.

CONFERENCE RESOLVES THAT:

Governments should establish, strengthen, promote and, where appropriate, constitutionally entrench anti-corruption entities that comply with the criteria noted in clause 5 above, both structurally and operationally.

In the formulation of policy and laws, corruption should universally be regarded as an infringement of human rights, which is both immoral and unethical.

Existing anti-corruption entities should be assessed and reviewed for their structural and operational compliance with the criteria noted in clause 5 above for the purpose of making adjustments and reforms where they are required.

Greater protection and incentivising of whistle-blowers, whether or not they are employees, should be considered in order to fortify this important aspect of the combating of corruption through appropriate investigation, prosecution and punishment of the corrupt in both the private and public sectors.

The nurturing of anti-corruption entities, both in the state and in civil society, through public education and the stimulation of the necessary political will to regard corruption as immoral, unethical and as a crime that violates human rights and undermines constitutionalism, should be encouraged through all means available in all forms of media.

A sanctions system, such as that developed by the World Bank, should be considered for implementation at the level of national jurisdiction in relation to all public procurement in whatever sphere of government, including procurement by state owned enterprises.

The private sector and civil society organisations should be encouraged to adopt and implement anti-corruption compliance programmes as contemplated by the Organisation for Economic Co-operation and Development.

Governments should establish a framework for the open and comprehensive declaration of assets and interests by all political office bearers and public officials.

By promoting this resolution, Accountability Now is continuing its efforts to raise public awareness of the pernicious nature of corruption and the need to implement all the resolutions taken at the conference, not only in South Africa but everywhere.

As noted earlier, it continues to advocate the creation of an Integrity Commission, and has made representations to the National Assembly Select Committee on Constitutional Review with a view to stimulating the political will to break with the dispensation that has been in place since the Scorpions were disbanded. In our view, this can best be achieved by supplementing the Hawks (whose mandate is far wider than corruption) with a high-powered commission devoted solely to preventing, combating, investigating and prosecuting corruption in all its manifestations.

In Glenister II, the Constitutional Court provided the recipe for designing effective anti-corruption machinery of state. Derived from research conducted by the OECD (or the Organisation for Economic Co-operation and Development), it has been tried and tested in countries with far lower levels of corruption than South Africa. In terms of this recipe, the following five criteria (represented by the acronym STIRS) must be satisfied in order to deal effectively with corruption:

- Specialisation of dedicated staff, structure and operations;
- Trained operatives with the necessary forensic, investigative, prosecutorial and educational skills;
- Independence from political influence and interference, both structurally and operationally;
- Resources which are guaranteed and adequate for the task at hand at any given time; and
- Security of tenure of office for the personnel of the anti-corruption entity.

The Hawks do not measure up to these criteria, and will never do so while they are located within the SAPS, which compromises their independence and security of tenure of office. There are many illustrations of this, ranging from the dismissal of General Anwa Dramat to the repeated efforts to dislodge General Johan Booysen. Poor leadership choices have also affected the efficiency of the Hawks. The impacts of these factors are evident in the precipitous decline in rates of arrest, from 14 793 in 2010/11 to 5 847 in 2014/15. Indications were that this decline in productivity would accelerate in 2016.

There is no silver bullet for dealing with corruption. However, the creation of a new Chapter Nine institution that would slot in neatly between the Public Protector and the Auditor General would go a long way towards addressing the culture of impunity that has taken root in all spheres of government.

The Auditor General, whose office is tasked with auditing and reporting on the spending of public money, is the 'canary in the coal mine' when it comes to identifying where corruption is worst in financial terms. The main mandate of the Office of the Public Protector is to examine public maladministration. It does not prosecute the corrupt, but it does have the power to take appropriate remedial action suggested by the facts uncovered in the course of its investigations. This power is wide enough to refer instances of corruption to the criminal justice system, but due to poor relations between the Hawks and the Public Protector, this doesn't happen all that often. An Integrity Commission, clothed with the status of a Chapter Nine institution and led by a former judge, would have the gravitas to deal with the organised criminals who are running rings around the state's current anti-corruption machinery.

South Africa has good anti-corruption laws. In order to succeed in the war on corruption, those laws need to be properly enforced. The time for an Integrity Commission is now, the idea is right, and the will to make it happen can be created by the people through civil society institutions, faith-based organisations, commerce and industry, academia, and political parties loyal to the constitution. With freedom comes responsibility. Active citizens, not passive subjects, are needed to drive the reforms required to reverse corruption and restore our society to a state in which the human rights enshrined in our constitution will be lived out in practice.

Index

About the author

PAUL HOFFMAN was born in 1950 in Johannesburg on the wrong side of town. His primary education was at the local Mondeor Primary School, secondary at St Martin's School in Rosettenville and tertiary at Wits University, where he read for the BA LLB degrees while completing articles of clerkship with the legal firm Bowens.

In 1975 he relocated to Cape Town and worked for various firms of attorneys until he was called to the Cape Bar in 1980. His early published works include monthly audio tapes called *Current Law Cassettes*, a column on new legislation for *De Rebus*, the attorneys' magazine, and a prize-winning article on the reform of pupillage for *Consultus*, the advocates' magazine.

In 1995 President Nelson Mandela conferred silk (senior counsel status) on him and he served as an acting judge on the Cape Bench at the request of three successive judges president. In 2006 he retired from the Bar to start the Centre for Constitutional Rights and since 2009 he has been pursuing his passion for constitutionalism as one of the six directors of Accountability Now.

He still lives in Cape Town, beyond the lentil curtain in Noordhoek, where he takes his dogs on long beach walks and practices yoga when not exacting accountability.